The Gift of Underpants:

Stories Across Generations and Place

by

Neal Milner

TRUDY IS A GREAT ADVOCATE
FOR AN AUTHOR TO HAVE.
I HOPE YOU AGREE
WITH HER, BUT IN ANY
CASE, ENJOY.

Neal Milner

ISBN 10: 1491019069
ISBN 13: 9781491019061
Library of Congress Control Number: 2013913197
CreateSpace Independent Publishing Platform
North Charleston, SC

Versions of "Sound Effects," "Professional Courtesy," "Super Bowl *Yahrzeit*," "Bridging Troubled Waters," and "Jerry Seinfeld's Florida and My Hawai'i" were in *Jewish Magazine* (jewishmag .com). An earlier version of "Walmart Greeter" appeared in *Civil Beat* (civilbeat.com). "The Gift of Underpants" first appeared in *Honolulu Magazine*.

For Joy

Last night I dreamt I was returning
And my heart called out to you
But I fear you won't be like I left you
Me kealoha ku'u home o Kahalu'u
— Olomana, "Kealoha Ku'u Home o Kahalu'u"

A'feelu in gan aiden iz nisht gut tsu zein a'lein. (Even in paradise, it's
not good to be alone.)
— Yiddish proverb

It's the strangest thing. I have lived in a lot of cities, some of them for
substantial lengths of time, but I have never thought of any of them as
home. Then, the other morning, I woke up and realized that Las Vegas
has, indeed, become my home. Somehow, in the few years I have been
living here and traveling out of here, this most un-homelike of cities has
come to function for me as a kind of moral bottom-line — as a secular
refuge and a source of comforts and reassurances that are unavailable
elsewhere — as a home, in other words.
— Dave Hickey, "A Home in the Neon"

TABLE OF CONTENTS

The Gift of
Underpants

When people from Hawai'i travel, they take along huge amounts of food, not to eat but to give away. *Omiyage*, people here call this custom of the traveler bearing gifts. Getting gifts of food is especially precious to those who grew up in Hawai'i but who now live far away. Mango chutney, poke, and musubi trigger strong memories of the place they chose to leave but will always miss. Just a whiff or a taste evokes deep and powerful feelings of old times — of small kid time, as we say in Hawai'i.

When Jews come to Hawai'i to visit their families, these traveling food memories aren't musubi and poke. They're kosher hot dogs and bagels. Bagels are a little better in Honolulu than they were when we first moved here in the early 1970s, but the big old-fashioned kosher hot dogs are still as rare as musubi in Corpus Christi.

When we first moved to Hawai'i, my in-laws used to bring us these dogs on their visits from Miami. But Miami wieners were not authentic enough, not close enough to our Milwaukee roots. The hot dogs had to come from Milwaukee because my wife's family grew up there eating wieners that they bought wholesale from Joe Pass Distributors. So before his trips to visit my in-laws in Florida, Uncle Oscar would go to Joe Pass, which because it dealt only in wholesale could afford to stay in a bad neighborhood, and pick up a couple of dozen to take on the first leg of their zigzag journey to Hawai'i.

Oscar packed them in his Jew-from-Milwaukee *omiyage* box and brought them to Florida. The in-laws then stored the franks in their freezer to bring when they came to visit us in Honolulu, where they arrived with the hot dogs packed in dry ice, as hard and big as the billy club that Oscar needed to ward off the muggers around Pass's store.

Starting with their earliest visits to Honolulu, my family also brought me underpants. My mother had begun to gift me with underpants when I first moved away from home after college. At the time she worked at Gimbels in Milwaukee, so she could use her employee's discount, fifteen per cent off, not as good a deal as Oscar got from Joe Pass but better than retail.

Buying me underpants was nothing new to her. No matter how rebellious an adolescent male is, his mother still buys him his underwear. Breaking away from your parents stops at buying your own underpants. When your mind is only on sex, drugs, and rock and roll, you are not going to be checking your dresser drawer to see how many decent pairs you still have. James Dean in "Rebel Without a Cause" let his mother buy him his briefs. Natalie Wood loved him even more for this.

My mother knew what style I wore because I had been wearing boxers ever since a week after I marched with the Craig Schlosser American Legion Band in the July 26, 1956 American Legion Convention parade in Eau Claire, Wisconsin. I remember the exact date because of underpants. On that day, wearing briefs, I had an escape problem that began just as the band got into formation at the beginning of the parade. The binding on the bottom of the underpants had snapped. Now this was not exactly the Macy's Thanksgiving Day Parade. Still, hundreds of people had their eyes on me for the length of the parade while I played the first trumpet part to "The Red Cross March" and tried with quick, sneaky hand movements to push myself back in and avoid chafing. (*Mommy, look, that trumpet player is playing his trumpet with one hand. Oho look, Mommy. He's being naughty.*) The next time my mother did an underwear inventory I broke the news to her. I wanted boxers from now on. Never mind why.

And so it went into adulthood. Boxers and gifts, boxers and gifts. I moved first two hundred, then two thousand, then five thousand miles away from home; I had a son, then a daughter; I went from a used car, to a new car, to one used and one new, to two new; and my mother still bought me underpants. Time marches on though now at least when I marched along with it, I could play trumpet with both hands.

After we had lived in Honolulu for a few years, my in-laws replaced my mother as my underpants supplier. They also got them for me at a discount from the PX at the Opa Locka Coast Guard Base in Miami. These boxers were just what you would expect military underwear to be — no frills, no little hearts or macho animals. They were just plain white, with an official Department of Defense serial number stenciled on the elastic waist band ("Undergarment. Lower. Department of Defense. #3 zee-ro, zee-ro, beta, Charley, niner, niner, Frank, 8, zee-ro. Men's white, boxer, medium. Warning: use only for protection of pubic and anal regions.").

At the airport we'd park the car so that we can meet the in-laws at the gate. As soon as Grandma and Grandpa step out of the passageway, they spot their gifted and lovely granddaughter and grandson who have become even more beautiful, if that's possible, thanks to the Hawaiian sun. The grandchildren step forward and shyly present their grandparents with two plumeria leis they have made all by themselves, just as they learned in school. The grandparents hug their grandchildren, then their daughter and son-in-law. They can't wait to please their healthy, loving family. It's been too long, far too long, but all these thoughts of distance and loneliness melt when they see and they touch. Even before the luggage arrives on the carousels, Grandma and Grandpa take packages from their carry-ons. Books and toys for the grandchildren, expensive, duty-free perfume for their daughter. The son-in-law gets underpants.

They were as long and baggy as a rapper's shorts. When I rode my bike through the Mānoa Valley, low in the saddle to cut the wind, these not-so-briefs hung out of my riding shorts like the skirt of a bedspread, a billowy petticoat for the stylish, cross-dressing cyclist.

There is a big difference between a mother and a mother-in-law giving underwear. The mother has been doing it for a long time. She knows your tastes. But how would my mother-in-law know what to get? We weren't that free and easy with one another. For the first few years of my marriage, I did not talk to my in-laws unless I was looking directly at them so that I did not have to decide what to call them. Hey, Mother and Dad? Anne and Max? They were not about to ask me about size or style. You've got to be, like, really loose and easy with your son-in-law to ask him whether he dresses right or left and whether he likes the bulge

14

or the hang. Instead, they asked my wife Joy. Once they knew, they were not about to raise the issue again, so it was all white all the time.

Joy and I began to give the gift of underpants to our children after they moved far away to the mainland, first to go to college and then to settle. Before a trip to see our daughter in Oregon, Joy would pick up a few pairs of those Costco panties packaged in cylinder-shaped containers that look like something the KGB used to send secret messages. Before a trip to New York, we would buy four packs of underpants (Arrow. Designer Boxers Colored. #8848691) for my son, also from Costco but packed flat like an Arrow dress shirt we would not dare buy for him because who knew what shirt style he liked or whether he even wore dress shirts?

There is no sentimentality in underpants. Fruit of the Looms don't evoke memories of kissing Mom good-bye as she put a bag of home made chocolate chip cookies in your hands when you first went off to college. The gift of underpants survives because underpants are the comfort food of gifts. Like eating rice or mac and cheese or those chocolate chip cookies, the giving of underpants from one generation to the next is a calming and reassuring gesture.

Parents who live far from their children have no real idea what goes on with them from day to day. Their children have jobs the parents do not understand. Their children either spend too much money or don't make enough. For long distance parents, it's a world impossible to imagine on a good day. On a bad day it's possible to imagine it but only for the worst. This is nothing new. A hundred years ago Jewish immigrants sang a Yiddish song about their kids called "*Vost Kenst Du Makht? Es Iz Amerike!*" — "What can you do? This is America." What can you do? Not much. Cell phones, social media, Twitter, they are all supposed to help, but what they really do is give anxious parents more opportunities to worry. What isn't she really telling us?

Enter underpants, an anchor in the mysterious lives of your children, a lifeline you can throw out to them to make *you* feel safe. They switch jobs when you are against it. They can be gay, marry a *goy*, quit medical school, or decide to go to medical school at the age of thirty-something with two young kids still at home. They can become Buddhist, or scarier still, a Hasidic Jew and never eat in your unkosher home again. But they will still wear underwear. For a brief, powerful moment the givers of underwear can live with the illusion that their world and their children's overlap.

For the sons and daughters, accepting the gift of underpants is a safe, comforting way to acknowledge that it's still OK to depend on your parents for necessities. Taking six pairs of panties from her mother is a lot less threatening to a daughter's pride than asking her parents for a loan to pay off the money she lost when her stock options went south but her Mini Cooper payments did not. Or when she is forty, living thousands of miles away, and her job is pulled out from under her.

We gave our son in Brooklyn four pairs of Arrow Designer #8848691 boxers when he came over to the Manhattan apartment where we were staying. When he came through that door, it was the first time we had seen him in six months and the first time we had been to New York to visit him in three years.

It was a warm, sunny Saturday afternoon in June when the three of us left the apartment that day on our walk uptown to see "True West" at the Circle in the Square Theatre. The streets were crowded with shoppers and walkers, and pedestrian traffic jams formed at the traffic lights. Still, we were early so we stopped for a quick lunch at a coffee shop on Broadway. On the spur of the moment while we ate, Joy said to Greg, "Why don't you spend the night at our place tonight? Then we can all go to Brooklyn together tomorrow to see your new place."

"I would, but I didn't bring anything," Greg said.

"You've got your new underwear. That's all you really need," Joy answered.

So for that one night the three of us slept together in the same house again. For that one night his mother did not have to worry that while she and I were eating dinner in Honolulu, he was out God knows where in the middle of the raucous, New York night. For one day she could pretend that his life was still woven into ours. She could pretend that the world of new mortgages, new jobs, new girlfriends, and new schemes for downloading music off the Internet resembled the world of tax-sheltered annuities, prostate screening, and the Oldies Channel. For one moment she could harbor a wistful wish that the adventure was just beginning for us, as it was for him.

The Name Game: Hymie, Hymie, Bo Bymie

Hymie Bornstein, the son of Uncle Sam the butcher, was a skinny, smart, nearsighted Jewish boy from Milwaukee. Hyland J. Barnes, also a skinny, smart, nearsighted Jewish boy from Milwaukee, was also the son of Sam the butcher. That's because Hymie and Hyland were the same person.

My mother, Celia Himmelreich, who was Hymie's cousin, was the daughter of another Sam, this one a tailor. Sam's Celia had a cousin living a mile away from her, also named Celia Himmelreich, daughter of Uncle Itzeh the grocer. My mother Celia had a sister named Esther and a sister named Sondra. Esther and Sondra, like Hymie and Hyland, were the same person.

Before they came to America in the early 1900s, my family experienced their world through the sounds of Yiddish. Wars, famines, pogroms, spoiled children, spoiled herring, these were all discussed with guttural, spitty, expressive Yiddish sounds. The "ch" sound: *challah, shlecht*; "k," "sh," "ts."

Especially the "eh" sound. "Eh" as in the Jewish shrug — "eh." "Eh" as the parts of so many common Yiddish words: *shaineh, shmateh, kleineh, tanteh, bubeh, zaideh, groiseh, messhugeh*. In their *shtetl* in Latvia the Himmelreichs couldn't talk to one another without using "eh" over and over again. The names of Sam's brothers and sisters were Laybeh, Louyeh, Itzeh, Ida, Roseh, Dobeh, Dineh, and Hantzeh. Only my Grandfather Sam and one brother, Herman, were spared. My grandmother and her sisters from that same *shtetl* were Ida, Lena, and Hinda, all pronounced "eh."

In the Old Country the same names got used over and over again because, for better or for worse, life went around in circles. You live, you die, your children lived and died in the same place. Besides, living in a ghetto surrounded by anti-Semites, who are you going to fool by naming your child something that sounds different? You were Jewish, you couldn't imagine otherwise. Even if you could, what good would it do you?

These sounds were about all the immigrants took with them in the early 1900s when they came to America where life was not so predictable or circular. Only a small pool of names came over on the steamships. Both my grandfathers were named Sam, and there was also a brother-in-law Sam (Hymie's father). Sam Himmelreich married a woman named Ida, the same name as one of his sisters. That sister married her first cousin Herman, which was also the name of one of her Himmelreich brothers. That Himmelreich Herman married a Jenny, also the name of his brother Louyeh's wife. Uncle Laybeh married a Dora, the same name as my paternal grandmother. The pairs: Sam and Ida, Sam and Lena, Sam and Dora; Herman and Ida, Herman and Jenny, Louyeh and Jenny. Saturday afternoon tea and coffeecake at my grandparents could include two Sams, two Idas, and two Hermans out of the eight old-timers squeezed around the kitchen table with the help of folding chairs.

Even when the names were not duplicates, they clearly sounded Jewish and stayed Jewish, regardless of the official records. No one ever called Uncle Itzeh by anything but Itzeh. As far as I know, Uncle Itzeh never even had an American name. Laybeh had another name, Kalman, but no one ever used it. Kalman was a documents-only name that went missing for years until it popped up in his obituary. Louyeh was usually called his Old Country name Louyeh, sometimes Louie, but never Louis or Lou.

The sound of some of these immigrant names had a whiff of American glamour to them, like my Grandmother's sister Lena — Hymie's mother — as in the singer Lena Horne. But with a *Tanteh* on one end and a Bornstein on the other, our Lena had no name glitter at all. Try saying, "Oh, *Tanteh* Lena Bornstein, you sing so sexy, girlfriend," and you see what I mean. Jewish all the way, or, as the family would have put it, *Takeh* a *Yid* — a Jew for sure.

Still, new country, new sounds. All of the immigrants in my family learned English. Some got pretty good at it. But English was only for business, the *lingua franca* of the small shopkeeper in a mixed neighborhood. Yiddish remained their language of description and understanding. They still felt, and of course argued, in Yiddish. The "eh" sound became their filter between the old and new worlds.

Beginning in 1910 or so, when these immigrants began to choose names for their newborn children, the sounds of the New World began to rub off on them just a little. Their cautious attitude toward American names was much like their cautious attitude toward American food.

They chose names for their kids that were a little apple betty but mostly apple strudel. No one who gave their children names like Celia, Molly, Bell, Irving, or Esther had to worry about those old Jewish ladies sitting in a park, wearing house dresses and stockings rolled down to their ankles, shaking their heads and saying, "What kind of name is that for a Jewish baby?" These ladies could be tough judges, like *Tanteh* Lena herself, who did a lot of bench sitting and a lot of judging. Once, when a new mother bragged about her baby's looks, Lena said, "Yeh, it looks pretty, but Hitler should only have its brains." Lena named her two boys Hymie and Meyer.

Sam and Ida Himmelreich named their daughters Molly, Celia, and Esther, all *Tanteh* Lena approved. In fact these names were so comfortable to the Himmelreich ear that a whole bunch of brothers, sisters, and in-laws used the same names. They also copied other names from each other. Maybe the names had some American sounds in them, but the Himmelreichs were not ready to move away from the tradition of sticking with a few good names. My mother and her sisters all had exactly the same names as their cousins. My mother had three cousin Bells, a sister and a cousin named Molly Himmelreich, a sister and a cousin named Esther Himmelreich, plus that cousin with my mother's own name, Celia Himmelreich.

Things could get confusing. Both Celia Himmelreichs worked at the same department store at the same time. One of my mother's sisters, Esther Himmelreich, found herself every year in class with her cousin Esther Himmelreich. A teacher's nightmare — which is which on the attendance sheet? It was confusing for the families, too. Which Molly are you talking about who was the *klutz* who dropped the Indian Head nickel down the sewer? Which Bell took the streetcar alone for the first time? Which Esther had impetigo? The parents dealt with this confusion the same way they had solved so many problems in the past — through Yiddish. They used the "eh." The families distinguished between the Mollies by calling the younger and skinnier one *Kleineh* (little) Molly, and the older and fatter one *Groiseh* (big) Molly. Big Molly sounds like a black blues singer, doesn't it? They used the same words and sounds to solve the problem of the two cousin Bells. The short one was called *Kleineh* Belleh while the larger one was just plain Belleh, never *Groiseh* Belleh, probably because *Kleineh* Belleh was so short that, compared to her, anyone would be *groiseh*.

My mother's sister Esther Himmelreich did not want to deal with this *groiseh* versus *kleineh* business, so she changed her first name to Sondra. This early out-of-the-box choice was a precursor. Except for this Esther-now-Sondra the rest of the cousins did not do anything official about their names. Instead they called each other by more American-sounding names. Hymie was Hy, Nathan was Nate, Belleh was Bell, *Kleineh* Molly was Molly. These sons and daughters of immigrants read *Saturday Evening Post* and listened to Tommy Dorsey, Benny Goodman, and "One Man's Family." Most but certainly not all of their friends were Jewish. The cousins were immersed in American sounds outside the home, the sharp, punchy, one-syllable sounds like "go," "great," "Smith," "car," and "ham."

They began to change their names not out of shame but out of economic necessity. The changes were career moves to help them make it in the Land of Equal Opportunity where there was still not such equal opportunity if you were Jewish. You were not hiding from the Cossacks any more, but in the wider world it still made sense for Jews not to raise red flags with their names.

Med schools had quotas. So Louyeh's son Nathan and Itzeh's son Joe, the first college graduates in the family and from medical school yet, changed their names from Himmelreich to Hillrich and Himes. Doctor Nate Hillrich and Doctor Joe Himes. Good, crisp *goyischeh*-sounding names. No "ch's" or "eh's." The c-h in Hillrich is not pronounced "ch" as in Uncle Chaim, but rather "ch" as in "rich," which is what Nate hoped to get with his MD and a new name. Himes and Chaim may sound a little alike, but that guttural throat noise is the difference between a horse and cart in Latvia and a 1938 Buick touring car in a leafy Milwaukee suburb with no trolley wires.

The most creative name change was not a riff on Himmelreich. Hymie Bornstein changed his name to Hyland J. Barnes so that he could get a job as a newspaper reporter in anti-Semitic Wisconsin towns. The name was WASPy enough to put a "Sir" before it or an "Esquire" after it — Sir Hyland J. Barnes, Esquire — the stem of the J standing alone, straight and tall as the flag pole in the squares of the towns that didn't want no Jew boys like Hymie. At the same time the name maintained its Jewish roots. At its core Hyland was a Hy. As for Barnes, among Jewish name detectives, which included everyone in the family, Barnes was a name that could go both ways. In fact there were some Jewish Barneses in Milwaukee. A successful balance: The name could pass where it had to but also was *takeh* a *Yid*. After Hymie changed his name, the old folks still called him Hymie. His friends and cousins continued to call him Hy. Jewish shape-shifting.

In the 1940s and '50s when my cousins, brother, sister, and I were born, the naming rules changed as new judges, now in slacks even, replaced the judges in house dresses. None of us share names, and we all have sharp, plucky American ones — Mike, Mitch, Bob,

Jeff, Judy — names that fit right into our schools' Dick and Jane books. Put a "Hi" and "How are ya" around any of those names and they sounded terrific, right at home in Ogallala, Nebraska, Dallas, Texas, or in our new neighborhoods in Milwaukee where the people next door were as likely as not *goyim* and where only the old people spoke with an accent.

In the 1960s when my generation began to have children, we felt free to give them any names we wanted. But we had no need to hide our Jewishness, and no desire to hide our Americanness. To us, quotas were a thing of the past, something that our parents talked about as object lessons but we chose to ignore. Anti-Semitism was something that happened in Germany. So my cousins, brother, and I gave some of our children spunky, Dick and Jane names that our parents might have picked (Greg, Howard, Joanna) and others names that would have given Lena a fit (Jacques, Arielle, Heidi. Heidi? A German name after World War II, are you kidding?). But we also chose Old Testament names (Joshua, Rachel, Adam). No Itzehs or Laybehs, though, because we did not consider them names as much as sounds that triggered gently derisive stories about those immigrants.

But those old-fashioned sounds too are making a comeback. I have a friend, Robert, who changed his name to Baruch when he became a Hasidic Jew and moved from San Francisco to Crown Heights in Brooklyn. A Bob in the hippest city in America to a "ch" in a place that is a time warp still filled with Yiddish sounds.

And now my new granddaughter Vivienne. Her father, my son, grew up in Hawai'i. He and his wife wanted a middle name for her that said something about both her Jewish and Hawai'i origins, so they chose as a middle name Naomi, which means "beautiful" in both Japanese and Hebrew. Far from an "eh" sound, but a roots name nonetheless. Vivienne was born in Brooklyn where they now live, a mile or two from Baruch, and just across the East River from where Vivienne's great-great-grandfather Sam Himmelreich had his tailor shop before he left New York to reunite with his brothers and sisters in Milwaukee. A full circle in a little over a hundred years. American Jewish history in a name.

School Dances and *Shul* Dances

Pop music was appalling in the early 1950s. It was as if regiment after regiment of promising singers and songwriters had gone off to Korea and had never come back. Elvis was still an unknown white kid listening to Negro music. Rhythm and blues? Who knew? The earliest rockers like Bill Haley and the Comets were still a few years away. Instead we got copycat crooners and vanilla swing. The Chordettes, who were from Sheboygan just up the road from Milwaukee, wanted Mr. Sandman to give them a boyfriend who looked like Liberace. Patti Page waltzed about buying a dog in a window, and Eddie Fisher crooned about his oh so wonderful papa.

Music was not rebellion the way it was with swing in the '30s or rock and roll later on. When I was in junior high, the same music was popular with both parents and their children. Take Eddie Fisher's "Oh, My Papa." It's a crisp fall night, a harvest moon, a small, cozy, basement rec room party, the parents watching "Your Show of Shows" upstairs and fighting the temptation to make sure every-thing's okay down there, while two fourteen-year-olds are dancing with their eyes closed to a tune featuring how terrific a guy's dad is.

Since we listened to our parents' music, we learned our parents' dances. But dancing was not one of the things that Jewish adolescents in Milwaukee wanted their parents to teach them. Dancing was too sensitive. It had a murky, sexual side that could cross dangerous boundaries between mother and son. There was no way I was actually going to hold onto my mother, touch any part of her clothing where I might feel her underwear, or, God forbid, dip her. So my friends and I paid to take dancing lessons. From a Jewish adult, but at least he was not one of our parents.

Because the instructor was parents-approved, what we learned was *shul* dancing, the kind of perky, chaste steps appropriate for weddings, bar mitzvahs, and, most of all, B'nai B'rith Youth Organization affairs. These were *shul* dances because they were held in places where Jews also worshipped, like the Beth Am Center and Halevi Hall, in a classier synagogue a mile away. We danced where we prayed. Saturday morning you would be saying Kaddish, and by that Saturday night you were doing the cha cha to "Cherry Pink and Apple Blossom White" on exactly the same spot.

These were also *shul* dances because these "affairs," as we called them, had such a clean-cut, model-youth, best-behavior vibe. These dances were instructional venues for proper teen age Jewish behavior — part of a homogeneity master plan so strong that it never needed to be made explicit. The B'nai B'rith Youth Organization's main objective was to keep eager, horny Jewish kids away from eager, horny gentile kids. After all, mixing could lead to sex or, worse, down the dark, disastrous domino path from contact, to "interdating," to intermarriage. Do I even have to mention that our parents had no trouble with this? Like the song "Poison Ivy," you could look, but you better not touch. In fact, come to think of it, maybe you shouldn't even look.

We took our dancing lessons at the neighborhood Beth Am Center, which was walking distance from our homes. Beth Am was simply a foundation of a building covered with a roof. The original plans were to make it a full time synagogue, but someone ran out of money, and construction stopped at the basement. So instead of a full time *shul*, this quirky, stunted building became a High-Holidays-Only place of worship, a semi-*shul*, but *shul* enough.

The other 360 days a year at Beth Am were open dates. So that place became a cheap rental space for all kinds of Jewish events, like wedding and bar mitzvah receptions, amateur stage shows, charity carnivals, my grandparents' golden wedding anniversary celebration, and B'nai B'rith Youth Organization dances. Cheap, rental, dancing space in a Jewish neighborhood — perfect for someone like Al Leeb, our instructor, who was trying to pick up a little extra cash by teaching clumsy, eager Jewish junior high students to dance.

There was nothing special about Al's looks. He was average height, thin, with wavy hair, and dark framed glasses on his long nose. His voice was nasal, slightly on the high side. Al could easily pass for an insurance agent, which he was in his day job. But when the music began, it was as if a shock jolted his body, making him smooth and elegant. Al seemed to get taller as he glided around the room, first showing the step by himself ("forward, side-together, back, side-together forward, side-together back"), then taking the hand of one of the girls in the class and sweeping her toward him. Suddenly she, too, was gliding across the floor, lost in the light, smooth motion, no longer remembering that she's dancing with a *nebbishy* Jewish insurance man old enough to be her dad.

When the boys actually had to take a partner and practice, all stiffness broke out. Our bodies always moved like we were

29

counting on our fingers, like we were picturing a dance-step diagram in our heads. My left arm constantly moved up and down to the music, taking my partner's arm along with me as if I was fetching a pail of water. The boys stared at our feet like we were trying to hypnotize them into obedience. We never smiled when we danced. No, sir. This was work. People don't smile when they are solving an algebra problem.

Whichever Latin dance we were doing, our upper bodies stayed ramrod straight. *Gringos* with back problems. A five-foot, two-inch, hundred-pound boy who had trouble keeping his laces tied counting in his head to the "Blue Tango" and dancing with a lanky girl four, five, six inches taller whose sudden growth spurt made her legs look as if they came out of her shoulder sockets. *Elegante, muy elegante.*

Still, after twelve lessons Leeb succeeded in teaching us the basics. For that he deserved much credit, but he had his limits. Al was smooth but he was *shul* dance smooth. Leeb taught us our parents' dance steps in the same Jewish venue where we would be using them. It was a dress rehearsal for propriety. He was an unofficial but potent B'nai B'rith Youth Organization outreach worker whose mission was to get us to keep the faith and keep it in our pants. What he taught us was nothing less, but nothing more, than the B'nai B'rith Youth Organization canon.

This was a problem because *shul* dancing was much less than what we needed. The Jewish social network was suffocating, but it could not operate twenty-four hours a day. There were no Jewish day schools in Milwaukee so all of us went to public schools where most of the students were not Jewish.

The adults who organized the school dances had no interest in keeping Jews away from gentiles. School dances were organized with a different mission: to keep everyone, regardless of color, race, or creed, out of mischief. These dances were held during the lunch hour in order to keep us off the streets. The theory was that light genital contact through clothing posed less of a risk than angry calls from neighborhood merchants complaining about swearing, smoking, and shoplifting.

At junior high school dances we were around people we never saw at Halevi Hall or Beth Am: mean, tough guys in greasy duck tail hair cuts and rolled up sleeves, the smokers — the "bops," as we called this collection of young rebel studs. Then there were the girls who over the summer had totally changed shape, wardrobe, and attitude. *Wow! Titties! Was that who I think it is? When did she learn to walk and talk like that?*

So school dances offered a whole different set of opportunities. They also created a whole different set of challenges. Dancing was different in school than in *shul*. Ballroom dancing was acceptable in school, but that was a small and dull part of an expanded dance package. To be a successful big time school dancer, we also needed to know how to do the jack, the slow dance, and the polka. These three dances were the difference between being cool and being a dink. Al Leeb did not teach us a single one.

The jack was dancing's Dark Side. Jack partners did not touch, but their not-touching was a kinky, sexy kind of not touching. Jack partners circled each other like exotic birds in a mating dance. Their bodies swayed with a little herky jerky thrown in. Fingers snapped. Jackers moved up and down off their toes, leaning *way* forward then *way* back with expressions on their faces that said, "There's a cigarette between my lips."

Where did they learn this un-Leebish dance? On their afternoon paper routes while us Jewish guys were at Hebrew School? No jacker would admit to learning it anywhere because the mystique

31

of the dance was that it looked like you did not learn it at all but were just doing what comes natural to you, snap, snap, Cool Daddy Cool. Asking some big tough guy standing next to his girlfriend with his collar up and his pants low, "Hey, Skipper, who taught you how to dance like that?" was asking for a trip to the school nurse.

The most important thing to know about the jack is not how it was done but who did it. Jews never did. At school dances the Jewish kids joined the circle of envious shy people, band nerds, Latin Club members, and clumsy growth-spurt oafs watching the bops do the jack with mean, tough, sexy girls wearing long, tight skirts and sweaters with the sleeves rolled up.

There was also a circle of envious bystanders at *shul* dances, but these circles were made up of proud, grinning youth group advisers and "teens" in modest spaghetti straps and sensible sport jackets watching Al Leeb's best pupil jitterbug with his cute date from a fancy East Side suburb.

The slow dance … the slow dance wasn't so much a step as an attitude, a combination of hormones and nerve. The basic slow dance step was the same as the fox trot box step that Al Leeb had taught us. But, as a whole package, the difference between the fox trot and the slow dance was the difference between me dancing with my cousin Marsha while her grandmother *Tanteh* Lena watched from her assigned bar mitzvah reception table and me dancing with my fantasy girlfriend in one of those nasty, wonderful, male adolescent dreams.

Al Leeb was going to teach us the slow dance? What could he possibly, possibly say?

Okay, everyone, time to learn the slow dance. Now, I want the girls to thrust your fresh, pouty breasts right into your partner. Hard. Real hard. Girls, you should feel those titties squeeze.

Now boys, shove your crotch right into your partner's pelvic area. Closer, still closer. That's it. You should be touching ... right there. Now, both partners, put your hands on each other's firm, ripe buttocks, keep them there, and move your fingers slowly, very slowly in circles. Close your eyes, and, girls, put your head on your partner's shoulders. Okay.

Oh, that's real nice, Aaron. Perfect! Everyone, see? Aaron has an erection. Boys, follow Aaron. Now, everybody, move and rub slowly — forward, rub, grind, side-together, back and rub ... Joyce, maybe it would be better if you took your glasses off. Aaron, keep it up. Now let's try it again. And...

We had the hormones and the steps. We just did not have the nerve. Slow dancers at school affairs ran the risk of getting interrupted by the vice-principal, Mr. Ayelward, who would shout from his spy perch in the gym balcony, "You two down there, yeah you, the ones dancing next to the medicine balls, give it more space, and I mean now, or I'm coming down there to do it myself!"

At school dances, some, the slick ones, the bops, took their chances with Mr. Ayelward. They got away with some stuff. So you got caught, big deal. A detention was a small price to pay for copping a feel. We, the future doctors, dentists, lawyers, and professors, who at thirteen were already worried about the damages that a soiled Permanent Record would do to our chances of getting into college, just looked on and dreamed.

Slow dancing was also risky at *shul* dances where vice-principals were replaced by, say, *Tanteh* Lena. Imagine a bar mitzvah party for *Tanteh* Lena's grandson Marty. I'm slow dancing with Marty's knockout sister, my second cousin Marsha, her slim, perfectly sculpted body pressed against mine, those dark, dark, brown doe eyes closed in ecstasy, my hands feeling the outline of her lace panties as her elegant, long fingers with that hot pink nail polish … Hmmm. Never mind. If I had tried it, if I had danced any closer with Marsha than I had danced in a mandatory trip around Halevi Hall with one of my aunties, *Tanteh* Lena would have been all over me like horseradish on *gefilte* fish.

Polka had real possibilities. It was easy to learn. Lessons weren't necessary. You needed enthusiasm instead of grace. And it was fun. People in my school polkaed at school dances. The dance was very useful because with all that frenzied bouncing and hopping, you were too busy to have to make small talk with your partner. So why didn't Al Leeb teach us the polka?

Because for Jews the polka was the quintessential *goyischeh* dance. Whenever I said something to my mother about doing the polka, she would say "yecch" as if I had told her I had gotten a job as a ham taster. Jews associated polka with the smell of stale beer; with weekend-long wedding receptions in bowling alleys; with mounds of cheap, unkosher cold cuts, bad pumpernickel bread, and smelly cheese; with fat, coarse people named Stosh or Butch, or Dottie. And especially with Nazis.

So for me, dancing the polka was a rebellion, not exactly like doing the jack with my cousin Marsha while holding a Lucky Strike in my hand and blowing smoke rings in *Tanteh* Lena's face, but then again I was not exactly James Dean. If a polka was playing during a school dance, and if I felt a little frisky, and if I could corral a little Jewish — or gentile — filly, I would roll out the barrel and have a barrel of fun.

But at a *shul* dance, the combo never played a polka, and no one ever asked.

The Last Breakfast

As the sun rose on a chilly Easter morning, three Jewish trumpet players played fanfares and flourishes celebrating the Resurrection of Christ. Dick Silberman, Larry Greenberg, and I had been hired for five bucks a pop to play the Easter services at Milwaukee's Ascension Lutheran Church, the largest Lutheran church in Wisconsin. We were the *Shabbos goys* in reverse.

Ascension Lutheran was on the other side of town, the South Side. Jews, like our three fathers, did business on the South Side but did not live there. The South Side was Polish, German, and Italian, with small pockets of Mexicans and Irish. It was heavily Catholic and Lutheran, all *goyischeh*. There were no synagogues there, no Jewish bakeries. For some reason, most of the Jewish cemeteries were on the South Side, fine for eternal but not for material life. The three of us had no friends on the South Side. The only time we crossed the viaducts to that side of town was to watch our high school play football against South Division or Pulaski.

As Dick's '55 Olds crossed that bridge over the Menomonee Valley, we could see the dim shadows of Milwaukee's industrial muscle, the factories that made the city a working man's kind of town in the 1950s but a rust belt failure less than twenty years after that. Easter Sunday or not, smoke rose from the stacks in the valley below. Harnischfeger, Falk, International Harvester, Allen-Bradley, Red Star Yeast, all surrounded by miles of Milwaukee Road rail track. If you carried a lunch pail and liked a shot and a beer after work, there was a good chance that you worked in sight of this bridge. Ascension Lutheran Church was just a mile south on a boulevard with substantial houses built when the middle class was still willing to live near factories.

Playing in a religious setting was strange to us. We never played our trumpets for Jewish services where the only wind instrument ever to make an appearance was the *shofar* three times a year. When we arrived at the church, we climbed the steps to the balcony and set up alongside the huge organ pipes near the choir. It took us just a few minutes of warm-ups to hear how well churches and trumpets go together.

We only had those few minutes because, to our surprise, the service started right on time, and with a full house. The Jewish services that the three of us attended never began with a full room. The only people who ever showed up at the starting time were the rabbi, the cantor, the sexton, a few synagogue big shots, and maybe a kid still basking in his post bar mitzvah conscientiousness. On Yom Kippur, when services lasted for hours, my synagogue looked like a department store during a fall sale. There were the few hard core shoppers who were waiting when the doors opened, a lot more who came about ten o'clock as the parking lot began to fill, and then a steady stream of customers going in and out of that prayer department store the rest of the day.

But at Ascension, by six thirty in the morning the place was filled. The minister suddenly pops out of the wings, the organist hits a chord, the chord cues the guy in the balcony, and the balcony guy cues us. It was like network television. And everyone stayed to the end. Why not? The service was so short that no one had time to get restless. "Who can worship without restlessness?" I thought as I watched this smooth operation taking place below. To me, restlessness was as much a part of worship as reflection and revelation. After an hour, a typical Saturday morning service at my synagogue was not even close to the halfway mark. At the Ascension Easter worship, people did not just stay. They also focused on the business at hand. There was none of the whispering, chatting, and schmoozing that we experienced at Jewish services.

Ascension was prompt, decorous, and, most of all, choreographed, from beginning to end. It was choir up, choir down; organ up, organ down; trumpets up, trumpets down; congregation up, congregation down; minister up, saying "this is the message of the Resurrection" … and 2-3-4, minister down, worshippers up and out, organ plays, doors close. Roll the credits. Sixty minutes on the dot. On to breakfast.

Between the sunrise service and the two later services, which we also had to do, the three of us were invited to a breakfast in the social hall with people who had attended the early worship. I was very hungry. All I had eaten for my predawn breakfast was a quick matzoh sandwich. Matzoh because that year Easter Sunday fell during Passover.

The food in the social hall smelled wonderful. Our hosts sat us at long party tables surrounded by generous strangers who wanted to make sure we ate our fill. "Great job, boys. Eat up. You deserve it. You got two more services to go," a kitchen volunteer said as she handed us plates of ham and eggs with toast.

Everything on those plates of course violated Jewish dietary law. These parishioners probably did not know that we were

37

Jewish, but even if they had known, they would have kept the same breakfast menu. What did they know about kosher or for that matter about Passover? This was the South Side. The closest Passover observers were close to ten miles and a cultural chasm away. People at the church may have known about the link between the Last Supper and Passover. Some may even have gone to a church Seder, but those celebrations were much more Last Supper than Passover. Maybe there was matzoh on the Christian table, but that was it. No one was going to say to the hostess, "Sorry, Mrs. Jagermeister, you can't serve that because the Jell-O and fruit cocktail weren't certified by a rabbi as Kosher for Pesach. And aren't those your everyday dishes you're using?"

I was caught between being Jewish and being polite — well, if not polite, then at least pragmatic. It wasn't that I was generally so much a keeper of the faith. I violated Jewish dietary laws all the time. Years before, my mother had begun buying all of our meat at the A&P after one too many complaints about the quality of the product at *Tanteh* Lena and Uncle Sam's kosher butcher shop. My grandparents pretended that they did not know this. Very little of the food was Kosher for Passover at my grandparents' family Seders, which were truncated mini-Seders consisting of a couple of opening blessings, the Four Questions, and one chorus of "Dayenu." Even then, the three brothers-in-law complained that my grandfather took too long.

Still, Passover ratcheted up my observance. Like almost every other Jew I knew, I had my own Unofficial Dietary Laws. These were not so much kosher-lite as kosher-imaginative. These unofficial laws had no theological basis; they were erratic, inconsistent, and hypocritical. That's what made them so effective.

According to my own rules, the Easter breakfast toast was definitely taboo. Giving up bread on Passover was the minimum marker of a good Jew. Eating bread on Passover was the surest sign of the devil's work, an unmistakable signal that this eater did not care, like a 1950s Catholic barbecuing a porterhouse steak on his parish priest's porch on a Friday night. Munching on a grilled cheese on white during Passover showed that you were an all around shirker and rebel — that your fast on Yom Kippur would end by eight o'clock in the morning if it even got started at all.

As for ham, even though my family did not keep kosher, there were never any pork products in the house. Technically pork is no more a violation than, say, unkosher hamburger meat, but try telling that to my parents or, for that matter, to any Jewish person I knew. According to this powerful unofficial law, unkosher pig is many orders of magnitude worse than unkosher cow. Period. End of story. But it was not really the end of story either for my family or myself. I ate bacon in restaurants. A pepperoni and sausage pizza was my regular choice. In fact, whenever we were at a pizza place after a Friday night football game, the Jewish guys ordered the pepperoni and sausage combo while our pre-Vatican II Catholic friends abstained. Out of the house my parents also ate bacon, particularly when it was concealed by lettuce and tomato and called "club." They especially liked spare ribs that they got at a restaurant called Pappy's, which was owned by a Jewish ex-pro football player named Buckets Goldenberg.

But never ham. Ham was special because ham separated Us from Them. Worse than unkosher, ham symbolized the Essence of *Goyischeh* Lifestyle, along with beer and drunken louts who stumbled around Wisconsin's North Woods with guns so they could bring Bambi home tied to the roof of those cars of theirs with the gaudy fender skirts and the false idols bobbing up and down on their dashboards. To tell you the truth, I liked ham. I never ordered it in restaurants but gladly ate it in the homes of my gentile friends. But not on Passover. According to my own rules, on Passover I had to try harder to be an Us rather than a Them. Ham was out of the question.

Eggs are a staple of the Jewish diet. Whenever we went on family picnics, my grandmother would add a couple of dozen hard boiled eggs to her picnic basket to tide us over in case we ran out of other things she brought for us to eat, which was about as likely as the Red Sea parting a second time. Still, you never can tell. And you wonder why open-heart surgery has joined *bris*, bar mitzvah, wedding, and burial as stages in the life of the Jewish male. Eggs are absolutely crucial for Passover. At a Seder, you dip them in salt water as a symbol of Jewish suffering. This ritual was so important that my Milwaukee family squeezed it into our in-by-six-out-by-six-thirty Seder. A hen can build a career out of laying eggs just for the Passover sponge cakes alone.

The problem at the church breakfast was not the eggs themselves but how they were served. The churchwomen volunteers brought us generous plates of food, Jewish in portions if not in content. In fact the plates were so full that the ham touched the scrambled eggs, which, according to my rules, caused severe egg pollution.

So there I was at the church breakfast, facing a tempting, forbidden feast with a growling stomach, a load of guilt, and two more services to go. If I had followed only that one set of unofficial laws, nothing would have entered my mouth. Fortunately there were two other unofficial rules I called upon that had nothing directly to do with Jewish dietary laws but everything to do with Jewish life. Let's call them The Two Pragmatic Laws.

Pragmatic Law I: *You got to eat something.* As in "You're leaving the house on an empty stomach? My God, you got to eat something!"

Pragmatic Law II: *Pick.* As in "Sol, honey, you just finished a big meal. Now with your lipids you're eating that piece of left over chocolate cake?" "Pearl, I'm not eating, I'm picking."

I ate something, but I picked. I took no toast out of the toast racks. Using my knife and fork like someone who had successfully pursued a career in the field of medical science, which by the way both Silberman and Greenberg later did, I carefully separated the innocent virgin eggs from the unclean seducer ham. With a flick of the knife I moved the meat to the very edge of the plate. I ate the eggs except for the parts that had brushed against the ham. To fill up, I emptied packets of strawberry preserves on the scramble — jam and eggs instead of ham and eggs. On the way to the garbage, I concealed the leftovers with my napkins, so that no one could see the uneaten food.

The three of us drove straight home after the last service. We did not stop to eat anywhere even though one of the best frozen custard stands in the city was a short distance from the church. Today, over fifty years later, I still have a much stronger memory of the food that day than of the music. Yet a few years ago, while leading my own family and friends' Seder in Hawai'i, I decided to give everyone a kazoo to use. At these Honolulu

41

Seders over the years people always seemed reluctant to express themselves. I wanted less decorum. I wanted them to sing out — hum out — rather than just politely and unemotionally read passages the way they usually did. So among other songs, we did many verses of "Dayenu" on an instrument featured in Jim Kweskin's jug band. It was far from the aura of trumpets at Ascension or the *shofar* at the end of Yom Kippur in *shul*, but still, the sound of the kazoo…

Sound Effects

In a surprisingly cheery Honolulu public library I am about to do story hour for about fifty children and their parents. Some kids quietly take seats next to their mothers or fathers while a few sit on the floor at my feet. Others scramble around, restless even before story hour begins. The area is a large open space surrounded by children's books, so there are plenty of chances to escape from listening to a much older and, for most, much whiter person, the children thinking, "That *haole* [Caucasian] guy, he's real old like Grandpa."

Sesame Street will not be hiring Mister Neal any time soon. I am not a hugger. My eyes don't twinkle. Children react to me the way they react to a large, unleashed dog shambling in their direction. The ones at my feet seem to be sitting farther away than they do when the children's librarian does story hour. And I am new to this, so I have none of the usual storyteller props: no chant, fish hook necklace, guitar or native flute, no wide red farmer suspenders. It's just me, clean-shaven, in my Gap Levi's 501s and fitted black Banana Republic tee.

I'm at this library today to tell only Jewish stories. "The Jews are here!" the librarian says to me, excitedly pointing to twin boys and their naval officer father who is stationed at Pearl Harbor. They are the only Jewish people in the audience.

My mother used to sing American nursery rhymes to me in Yiddish, translating them on the spot. "Three Blind Mice" became *Drei bleender mizelech, drei bleender mizelech/dee moiz iz gelofen un der zayger, dee moiz iz gelofen un der zayger*. Peter, Peter was a *keerbus esser* who *hawt a vibe une err ken neet farzorguen*. Although I did not understand Yiddish, that version was much funnier to me. To a five-year-old, Yiddish sounded like spitting, tongue-twisting, high-decibel hysteria.

In fact I was surrounded by live Yiddish nursery rhyme characters. I heard that language all the time because Yiddish was the mother tongue of my immigrant grandparents as well as their brothers and sisters. All of them got by in English, but Yiddish was their everyday language. It was the language of melodrama. In *Tanteh* Lena and Uncle Sam's kosher butcher shop Lena and her sister Ida, my grandmother, loudly argued over the cleanliness of the store's only meat grinder (*"You're crazy." "I can see chunks of meat hard and dark like coal!"*) in front of a live audience of customers in a room barely big enough to hold a butcher block table and a small counter. Adversaries about meat, the sisters were allies about tragedy. They wept loudly whenever Sam read aloud the sad stories in the Yiddish language newspaper *The Daily Forward*.

For those Jewish immigrants, Yiddish was, as it always has been, a marker of their outsider heritage. The nursery rhymes were an early reminder to me of who we were and how we were different. My mother was an accidental Yiddish folklorist. By translating the nursery rhymes, she did something that Jewish storytellers have done for centuries. She borrowed material from the dominant culture — The Historical *Goyim* — made fun of it, and made the blind rodents and pumpkin *fressers* our own. My mother thought she was simply keeping me entertained. In fact she was initiating me by letting me in on a historical inside joke.

That sort of joke works fine for a Jewish audience. Historically, that's why these jokes existed, a way for Jews to talk to each other about outsiders. But telling those jokes to the uninitiated is a different story entirely, and Honolulu is as uninitiated about Jewish life as an American city gets. It's a comfortable place for Jews, but people here have no experience with everyday Jewish life. Every Passover and Chanukah, the local newspapers run photos of some Jewish family happily eating something or lighting something. In a sidebar next to these photos there is Jewish festival news you can use, like recipes for making low-fat *latkes* or heart-healthy beef brisket with a zest. Who the hell uses these recipes? No one I know. And that's it.

"Do you practice?" people here sometimes ask me when they find out I'm Jewish. That question comes from a combination of ignorance, curiosity, and distrust reserved for fringe religions. No one ever asks a mainstream Protestant, "Are you a practicing Presbyterian?"

I got into Jewish storytelling in Honolulu because I was a white person who knew my place. When my friend the librarian invited me, she said by way of encouragement, "No one in Honolulu tells Jewish stories. The *haoles* always want to tell Asian and Pacific stories. I got plenty of those already." In other cities just a whisper of an invitation for Jewish storytellers would bring out long lines of eager volunteers, including many of my relatives, particularly my Uncle Hy, a pimp and slumlord who, considering his juice with the Milwaukee Police Department Vice Squad (its commander was a pallbearer at Hy's funeral), would have felt more than comfortable sharing his experiences and maybe even a little-black-book address or two. But in Honolulu I became the go-to Jew by default.

When I was ready to try my skills on adults, I wrote a story about name changes in my family, like Hymie Bornstein (Lena and Sam's son) becoming Hyland J. Barnes. I worried that my Honolulu audience would not understand the real significance of the changes in the sounds of the names. My librarian friend, who is a gifted local storyteller with a national reputation, told me not to worry about getting deep. "Just concentrate on the sounds," she said reassuringly. "The Jewish names sound so musical, like Hawaiian." Now, the name Alani Keliʻihoʻomalu Kamakawiwoʻole comes out a little different than Yankl Teitelbaum, but I knew what my experienced friend was going for, and who was I to doubt the power of Jewish sounds?

Still, I understood that the sounds alone tapped into only a small part of the full story about Jewish names. To the uninitiated like a Hawaiʻi audience, Himmelreich to Hillrich to Himes sounds like a double play combination with a Prussian shortstop. To people whose families had lived these experiences, these changes were the opening pages of a rich archive of lived or remembered experiences and symbols of immigrant twentieth century Jewish life: going from a small Milwaukee shopkeeper from Latvia who kept his store open on the Sabbath to support his family; to a student at a third-tier med school that did not have a Jewish quota, especially if you Anglicized your name; to a successful physician whose own children could do what they wanted without worrying about anti-Semitism or money, or, for that matter and for better or worse, not think about being Jewish at all. After I told this naming story at a Lion's Club lunch meeting in downtown Honolulu, the mayor's wife came up to me and said, "I didn't know that Cohen is a Jewish name."

Word about me got around. Actors who were rehearsing for a staged reading of "Angels in America" asked me to teach them how to pronounce the script's Hebrew, the Mourner's Kaddish. The Kaddish is full of pesky, unfamiliar "kh" sounds: *V'yamlikh malkhutei b'chayeikhon uv'yomeikhon...* English has no "kh" sound. What's more, Hawai'i has an unusual number of "k" sounds — surnames, place names, close to 1,500 street names that begin with "k," but nothing close to "kh" sounds. Without coaching, the "k" sound filled the vacuum. My job was to convert "k's" to "kh's."

Some teacher. Like most of my friends, I hated Hebrew School and skated by. Fifteen days, seven hours, and thirty-eight minutes after my bar mitzvah, when Hebrew School ended for the year, I was gone for good. I can pronounce Hebrew well enough to pray in the language, but I never picked up the minor frills like speaking it. My vocabulary is so limited that the only two sentences that I can put together in Hebrew are, "Hello, Jewish National Anthem. My mother is my father." That was a high enough bar for the actors. The actors and I co-existed on two separate paths that converged momentarily over sounds. For them, the Mourner's Kaddish was about the script. For me, it was about the death of my father.

At another library story hour I told the children a Hasidic folktale called "The Nigun."[1] In Hebrew, *nigun* means melody,

---

[1] From "Jewish Stories One Generation Tells Another," as retold by Peninnah Schram (Northvale, NJ: Jason Aronson, Inc., 1993, pp. 369–75).

particularly a wordless melody. Hasidic Jews believe that the human singing voice is the purest, most direct way of communicating with God and that melodies with wordless, spontaneous sounds are the purest of the pure. The singer uses any sounds that happen to move him. Typically the sounds resemble Yiddish.

That *nigun* tale is about a poor but scholarly young man named Hayim. His rich future father-in-law, Yankev Ben Moishe, sends Hayim to the city with a hundred rubles to buy satin for the wedding coats. Instead of spending the money for the satin, the young man becomes so enraptured by two shepherds' flute melodies he hears along the way that he gives the herders each fifty rubles to teach the melodies to him so that in his voice each will become a *nigun*. Hayim comes back to his village ecstatic but satin-less. His future father-in-law thinks the boy is an irresponsible nutcase, and the match between Hayim and the daughter goes kaput. Feeling not at all jilted, Hayim says to himself, if Mister Big Shot Yankev Ben Moishe wants to dump me, fine. I got me two new *nigunim* for the Sabbath, and now I can find a truly pious wife and father-in-law who understand that two ecstatic new paths to God are worth infinitely more than some shiny, high-class fabric.

The sounds of the *nigunim* are the heart of the story. The melodies appear again and again. First one melody, then the other, then the two *nigunim* one after the other, then more. Though the melodies are written in the text, the teller makes up the wordless sounds. As I prepared this story, the songs took over. They enraptured me, too. I did not think about which sounds to use. They just emerged. The more I rehearsed, the more they pulled me in. I sang them over and over, much more than I needed to. I found myself humming them at odd times and places. When I rehearsed in my tiny study, my body moved like ecstatic Jews in prayer have moved for centuries:

*La **di** da da **di** da da*
*Voy voy voy la di da **di** da da.*
***D**i da da **di** da da*
*Dai dai dai dai di da **da**.*

That's what I sounded like and looked like when I told the story at the library. The children responded just as I did. They sang along loudly with each *nigun*, their bodies swaying each time more enthusiastically after each chorus, as if they did not want the story to end. All of us in the large, airy room were united by the sounds.

But just by the sounds. Their swaying and singing came from watching me. My swaying and singing came from memories and layers of my own personal experiences: living nursery rhyme characters; my mother's voice; old women wailing *ai, ai, ai* at Yom Kippur memorial services; B'nai B'rith Youth dances; my family's dislike of the Hasidic Jews in our neighborhood; Hasidic folk tales; Woody Allen's parody of Hasidic folktales; growing up in a neighborhood where many of my friends went to Catholic schools; and, most of all, the intense, complicated mixture of attachment and detachment that I feel living in Hawai'i.

Perry Como taught my family how to mingle Jewish traditions with the outside world. In the 1950s, Como, who was not Jewish, was huge, *huge*, as big as Milton Berle. The crooner recorded a version of "Kol Nidre." His version has a gauzy, vapid, laidback sound, which works for "Papa Loves Mambo," but "Kol Nidre" begins, "From this Day of Atonement I shall repent," and then gets even deeper. Any decent cantor's "Kol Nidre" on Yom Kippur blows Perry's version out of the water. No matter. Como's "Kol Nidre" was a smash. My mother and all my relatives loved it. I'm sure it made *Tanteh* Lena cry.

They loved it precisely because it was so Comoish, which to them was an honor. *Tanteh* Lena, my grandmother, and all the rest of those immigrants and their children knew that neither "Kol Nidre" nor Yom Kippur touched Como personally the way it touched them with deep feelings of repentance, loss, and memories of the Holocaust. To them, there was "Kol Nidre" the prayer, and "Kol Nidre" the song. Perry's was the song, and that was fine. They saw the recording as a sign of recognition and respect. "Kol Nidre" is said in the synagogue only once a year, but my family could hear Como's version on their Victrolas any time they wanted. Playing the record was a constant reminder that that famous crooner took an interest in their lives.

In Hawai'i, people take an interest in my life. Being Jewish adds zest, recognition, and mystery to my whiteness. I may be a *haole*, but because of my stories I am not just a *haole*. Being someone with only partially understood stories is better than being someone with no stories at all. No librarian in Hawai'i ever says to a *haole*, "I need someone to do Caucasian stories. Tell them what it was like growing up rich and Episcopalian in Kenilworth, Illinois."

After one of my performances, a local guy, an Asian American who had lived in Hawai'i all his life, came up to me and said, "I had a *Tanteh* Lena too." We both laughed. He did not have to say anything more. I knew what he meant. My story linked us. It did what storytellers try to do, create a community with the audience. I appreciate the importance of this Universal Lena, just as *Tanteh* Lena had appreciated the value of the Universal Como.

But that universally shared Lena is only a fragment. I still hold onto my own personal *Tanteh* Lena. In that Hasidic folk tale about the *nigun*, Yankev Ben Moishe could not fathom the emotional core of Hayim's experiences no matter how loudly or passionately Hayim sang.

Hayim did not see this as a failure. On the contrary. Hayim saw his differences as a gift because they helped the young man reaffirm who he really was. And after all, Hayim also had other places to take his songs.

Music Appreciation

My grandfather Sam Himmelreich knew firsthand what each of his three son-in-laws did for a living. Sam lived in the same house as one son-in-law, my father Dave. We lived downstairs; my grandparents lived above. Six days a week he heard Dave get into his laundry truck early in the morning and return just before supper. On late Sunday afternoons, Sam watched Dave work at his cramped desk in the hall off the kitchen, bringing his customer records up to date and planning his route for the coming week. He heard Dave talking over the phone to angry customers whose spots had not come out and to deadbeats who wanted Dave to just leave the pants and get paid some other time. As Sam drank his final evening cup of coffee before going upstairs to his own place, he watched his son-in-law put the day's receipts into envelopes and hide them in a dresser drawer.

Sam knew firsthand what his son-in-law Donald did because Donald did it directly to Sam's body. Uncle Donald was his doctor. In fact, he was the whole clan's doctor. The family women went to Donald for some parts of the body but not for the women's stuff. Relative or not, free or not, they weren't going to let him do that to them down there. All of Sam's parts fit easily within

Donald's jurisdiction, so Don was his doctor all the time. Having a son-in-law touch your naked body and know things about your health that you would never tell your wife or children is as intimate and firsthand as it gets. Of course the older Sam got, the more time he spent with Donald. The two of them together made Sam's final decision. During his last days in a nursing home, Sam refused to eat. Donald was assigned to make one last attempt to turn things around. He brought Sam a corn beef sandwich and a pickle. "Look what I brought you, Pa. Your favorite food," Don said. Sam refused. "It's time," Donald told the family. "It's time."

Sam knew firsthand what his son-in-law Hy did for a living because after Sam retired from his tailor shop, Hy became Sam's boss. Sam worked as a part time cashier at Hy's discount store, Wholesale Merchandise Distributors. Three mornings a week Hy picked up Sam in a white Cadillac Coupe de Ville. They schmoozed away in Yiddish as the big Caddy with the fins cruised across the Menomonee Valley to Hy's store on the South Side, up the block from the Harnischfeger plant on National Avenue and a mile from Milwaukee County Stadium.

Wholesale Merchandise Distributors was a schlocky, miniature Walmart before Walmart was around. The entire store was the size of a Walmart customer service counter. Wholesale's three aisles were so narrow and so filled with goods that shoppers coming toward one another had to step sideways to pass. It sold cameras, perfumes, clothes, toys, stationery, watches, whoopee cushions, and anything else Hy could purchase by the gross for next to nothing. All this was sold to the customer at wholesale prices. At least that's what the store claimed.

Hy the schmoozer was also Hy the operator, the black sheep of the family who had deserted my aunt in a small Iowa town in the middle of the Depression, leaving her a destitute, lonely, solitary Jew in a sea of Norwegian Lutherans. Then a couple of years later he got her to remarry him. In the eyes of my family, including my grandparents, giving Hy a second chance was not such a good idea. Sam had very ambivalent feelings about Hy. Hy was in many ways the most generous of the sons-in-law. He had an easy way about him that made people, including my grandfather, feel comfortable in the moment — schmoozing in Yiddish. He took my grandparents on cross-country car trips, and Hy's job offer was exactly what an active person like Sam needed. But my grandfather knew about Hy's other side — the way he treated his troubled wife and children, his mysterious, shady, side businesses, the women he had on the side.

Hy needed watching, which is exactly what Sam could do from his cashier's perch in that tiny store. He knew when Hy lit his dollar cigar and when he just chewed it. He could hear when Hy haggled on the phone with some jobber in New York or with an anonymous person on a pay phone trying to unload a truckload of genuine Bavarian music boxes that may or may not have been his legally to sell. Sam saw Hy talk customers into spending a little more for a Christmas watch than they wanted or the watch was worth. And my grandfather knew when Hy mysteriously slipped out of the store without telling anyone where he was going or when he would be back.

Keeping tabs on his grandchildren was more complicated for my grandfather, especially after we began to go off to college starting in the late 1950s. We were now out of sight, not like Dave, Hy, and Donald. What Sam knew about college was this: You should go there. Anything else about it was a mystery to him. Still, he had lived in the same house with three of his grandchildren for many years, and until they went off to college, he saw the rest of them all the time. Sam could only imagine college life, he could only imagine his grandchildren's future, but he had a base. He did not have to imagine their past because he had lived it with them. In fact, the grandchildren's futures turned out to be well within the imagination of a self-schooled immigrant who had been in America long enough to know where the money, prestige, and good deeds were. We became college professors, health professionals, social workers, lawyers, and business people — solid Jewish professions. He did not live to see most of this, but had he lived, he certainly would have had a good idea of what we were like and what we were doing.

So different from the connections between my two children, Greg and Joanna, and their grandparents. When it came to my children, their grandparents could *only* imagine their grandchildren. They had nothing else to go on. My kids grew up in Hawai'i thousands of miles away from Milwaukee and South Florida and never lived near their grandparents. To their grandparents, my children were exotic, mysterious creatures whom they loved but could only learn about at a distance. A one-week visit here, a two-week visit there, that's about it for thirty years. Long distance phone conversations were no help. My son and daughter were always "fine" and school was "okay." Then an awkward pause, then "love you, put your mother on the line."

My mother-in-law was always so curious about what it was like to grow up Jewish in Hawai'i. Greg and Joanna never knew quite what to say about this. Their grandparents' frame of reference was the tight Jewish neighborhoods in Milwaukee where they had grown up and raised their children — Jewish organizations, Jewish functions, Jewish camps, Jewish friends, Jewish boys and girls to date.

My children sang the Hawai'i anthem, "Hawai'i Pono'ī," at the beginning of every elementary school day. Once when my mother-in-law asked what it was like being Jewish in Hawai'i, Joanna said, "Grandma, we don't think about what it's like to be Jewish. We think about what it's like to be *haole*."

My children went to college far from their grandparents, and took up professions that were well outside the Depression-era Jewish imaginary. A few years after her college graduation my daughter announced that she was giving up her good, steady, full time job to work as a temp because she wanted the flexibility to travel more. To grandparents who had lived through the Depression, temps were hobos who rode the rails and asked farmers if they could spend the night and work for food. Joanna might as well have sung the Wobbly anthem, "Hallelujah, I'm a Bum." Four years at an excellent liberal arts college, and she decides to be the kind of person Woody Guthrie sang about?

It was even harder for the grandparents to imagine what my son Greg did after college when he became a writer and editor for the music magazine *Spin*. At the time, *Spin* had a circulation of over a half-million readers, it's safe to say none of them over eighty years old. *Spin* paid as much attention to the elderly as AARP does to hip-hop.

Spin was full of articles about music and groups that older people had never even heard of enough to hate — Rage Against the Machine, Slint, A Tribe Called Quest, The Notorious B.I.G. The magazine's stories went up the page, down the page, across the page. They scrolled in very small print along the bottom. The print size and color changed from one line to the next. Bifocal hell. *Spin*'s ads were filled with pictures of skinny, tattooed people in baggy *shmatehs* who, it turned out, were actually modeling those *shmatehs*. A "Got Milk?" ad featured the rock group KISS in their full regalia with masks, saying, "Lick it up."

My mother was not totally un-hip to rock and roll writing before she first encountered *Spin* because earlier she had taken a ten-mile bus ride from her suburban apartment to a Sam Goody record store in a run-down inner city Milwaukee mall, where she had not shopped in years, to get a copy of a piece Greg had written for that record chain's magazine.

My mother did not have to work so hard to get *Spin*. She discovered it in the pile of magazines at her beauty parlor. What it was doing in that place was a mystery. This was not a hair salon. It was a beauty parlor. A salon has anorexic stylists in black unisex outfits shaving the heads of people with pierced privates. My mother's hair place was a place where, rain or shine, the customers put on plastic bonnets before they left the shop. Coming across *Spin* that way was like Dante's grandmother eight hundred years ago accidentally coming across a copy of Dante's "Inferno."

So that's what Dante's been up to! Hey, Signora Shapiroelli, take a look at what my grandson the writer has written. These words! "As I revolved with the eternal twins, I saw revealed, from hills to river outlets, the threshing-floor that makes us so ferocious." I think it's a story about good and evil, but I am not too sure. The important thing is that his name is on it. See? Right there. Dante.

My mother took *Spin* from the pile. First she checked the masthead and found his name. "Greg Milner, that's my grandson," she bragged to the beautician looking for my mother's honey brown rinse.

Under the hair dryer next to other grandmothers who were also there for their standing appointments, my mother began paging through the magazine searching for her grandson's article. The other ladies, relaxing in their pink smocks with their legs idly crossed, are looking at heart-healthy, meal-in-a-minute chicken recipes and magazine plot summaries for "As the World Turns." My mother's looking at bare-chested drummers and women in tight leather body suits on motorcycles.

After paging through the freaky ads, the eye-popping photos, and the splashes of color, she finally comes across her grandson's story about the band Fugazi.

So that's what Greg has been up to in New York City. Hey, Mrs. Shapiro, take a look at what my grandson the writer has written. These words! "With roots in harDCore heroes Minor Threat and emo-core pioneers Rites of Spring, Fugazi combines the rhythmic vigilance of Bad Brains and D.C. go-go with catchy Britpunk choruses, New Wave shimmy, and brutal guitar skronk." I think it's a story about music, but I am not too sure. The important thing is that his name is on it. See? Right there. Greg Milner.

My mother became a subscriber. Both sets of grandparents did. Greg gave them all subscriptions. *Spin* now had a half-million young readers and three old ones. No editorial changes were planned.

What connects grandparents and their grandchildren in a world so different from the one I grew up in? In the acknowledgements section of the book that Greg wrote about the heavy metal band Metallica, he had this to say about what makes that connection work: "The enthusiasm my grandfather, Max Primakow, had for this book, despite never having heard (or heard of) Metallica, made it easier to write, and I wish he'd had a chance to read it."

Enthusiasm. Enthusiasm was the glue bonding my children and their long distance grandparents. Expressing enthusiasm is not really about truth. It's a ritual. Rituals are not meaningful because they are accurate. They are meaningful because they are emotional links, from the heart rather than the head. In fact, the ritual of being enthusiastic works better at long distance where no one can see your face because seeing your face might give away what you are really thinking: *She quit her job to travel — and alone? He can make a living that way? She's single, and bought her own home.* My children knew there was some acting going on when their grandparents said they were excited about one or another of their grandchildren's undertakings. Their grandparents probably knew that Greg and Joanna knew. Still, this enthusiasm was a powerful link because fundamentally it signaled this: We love you, we trust you, and we care.

By the time Greg published his next book, which was a history of recorded music, three of his grandparents were dead, and the other was far too deep into dementia to understand. Not likely that the other three would have understood it had they still been alive. That book was a finalist for the National Book Critics Circle Award. His grandparents would have been enthusiastic.

Renewal

In my family's eyes, the small group of Hasidic Jews in our 1950s Milwaukee neighborhood was a bunch of ragtag, unruly fanatics always on the lookout for donations. They were the only Hasidic Jews in town, but for my mother they were more than enough. "Those Twerskis," she called them, referring to the Hasidic *Reb* Twerski and his followers. They were fools, a circus of furry eighteenth century clowns dressed in black. All that wailing and swaying. All those *oy oy oys* and *voy voy voys*. And the noise from the synagogue seats! There the chatter and gossip were as loud as the *davening*. While some prayed loudly and passionately to God, others talked just as loudly and passionately about their scrap metal business. When the noise got too loud, someone — anyone, everyone — would shout *"Sha!"* and things would quiet down for a few seconds. And prancing around with the Torahs on Center Street right in front of the Number 22 bus? Shouting, undulating, immersing, this was much too much. The Twerski synagogue had the only Mikvah, a ritual bath, in town. For the Hasids the Mikvah ritual was spiritually purifying. For my mother it was a filthy source of contagion and germs, something to add to her list of polio scares. And of course no one in the family ever went to the Twerski *shul*.

My grandfather and his brothers were immigrants from the same part of the world as the Hasids. Their history was the Hasids' history, and their reasons for coming to Milwaukee were the Hasids' reasons. But every *Shabbos*, the ultimate day in the week for prayer and rest when work was prohibited according to Jewish law, the Himmelreich brothers got up early to open their tailor shops, taverns, and grocery stores. For them *Shabbos* was a big day all right, but not a Hasidic sort of big day. A day of rest? Are you kidding? For the Himmelreich brothers Saturday was the big money day. Who could afford to close a store on the days when everyone else shopped?

When they went to *shul* on the High Holidays, the Himmelreich brothers could *daven* just as well as the Hasids. The prayers were the same for Those Twerskis and those Himmelreichs, but they sounded different. The Twerskis were *fortissimo*, emotional — exalting and extolling — calling out to God. The Himmelreichs' prayers were *piano* to *mezzo forte*, lukewarm — reciting and mumbling — hoping that God was processing for content, not for affect. The Twerskis shimmied and undulated at the mention of God. Sam and his brothers dipped their shoulders just enough to get by.

This was definitely not about assimilation. The Himmelreichs were certainly not any more tolerant of newfangled modern Jews. They looked down just as much on Those Reformed, as they called the reformed Jews, as they did on Those Twerskis. All the reform synagogues in Milwaukee were on the East Side, where the rich Jews lived and we didn't. There were no Orthodox *shuls* on the East Side. My mother had a long list of things that were wrong with Those Reformed: They prayed in English. They used an organ. They hired a choir in which *goyim* were welcome as long as they could do the gig. Their services were too short. They celebrated

Rosh Hashanah only one day. They wore no hats when they prayed. They did not keep kosher. These criticisms boiled down to this: too much fun, too easy, too *goyischeh*. All this from a woman who could not read a word of Hebrew, did not keep kosher, and did not go to *shul* even on the High Holidays. My parents were not members of any synagogue, and my father worked on Yom Kippur. But my mother did not need any bona fides to have her reasons.

Those Twerskis certainly were not too *goyischeh*. Oh my, no. But too much fun, too easy? In a way, yes. All that noise the Hasids made, it sounded like they were actually *enjoying* themselves in *shul*. And it went on every day like this, not just four times a year or fifty or so Sabbaths a year. A Hasid, you were a recognizable Jew all the time, just like in the old country. You wanted to be. My family certainly did not want to hide their Jewishness. Their Jewishness went far beyond self-conscious pride. To them, it was the natural order of things. They just did not want to advertise and be so immersed in it. Because the Himmelreichs had no experience with prayerful passion and ecstasy, they were certainly not going to approve of all that outrageous and alien enthusiasm.

But it wasn't just the fun. Those Twerskis were fanatics in other ways. Always with a million rules to cover everything, so overly kosher, and always asking their rabbi about every little thing. So, according to my family, the Hasids had too few rules and too many rules. Those Twerskis were too undisciplined, and they were also too disciplined. We had them coming and going.

Still, the Milwaukee Hasids were not exactly a looming presence. There was no Hasidic neighborhood in Milwaukee. Only Rabbi Twerski and his family actually wore Hasidic garb, less than ten people in all. The rest of their tiny congregation looked like the rest of us. Most of the time a person could walk up and down

Center Street and not see a single black hat. The Hasids were not part of my family's everyday life but still were a powerful part of their imagination and sense of what a Jew should be. They were more a part of my mother's imagined world than her real world.

The only house my parents ever owned, the one they lived in for over forty years, was a small, stone duplex that we shared with my grandparents on the West Side. Though this was a Jewish neighborhood by Milwaukee standards — the Hasidic *shul* was just a mile away — Jews were in the minority. Our neighborhood was full of Irish, Italian, and German families — cops, plumbers, tool and die makers, bus drivers, fire fighters, school teachers, a few other white collar workers. Chevys and Fords with an occasional Buick.

From the curbs, large elms shaded these modest homes with their meticulous yards. Meticulous, the patron saint of Milwaukee neighborhoods. Both total strangers and close neighbors judged you by how you kept up your lawn in summer and your sidewalk in winter. In winter, people didn't shovel their walks for safety. They shoveled for status because their moral standing depended on it. A yard that was out of hand was a sign that the people living there were out of hand. In summer the neighborhood was a carpet of closely clipped lawns, small, trimmed evergreen bushes, and neat — extremely neat — borders of marigolds, pansies, petunias, and geraniums. Letting crabgrass or dandelions grow on your lawn was like letting some crazy, wandering drunk sleep on your steps. The neighborhood was not all Jewish, but it was all white. White people judging white people. Milwaukee was one of the most segregated northern cities in the country.

Forty years later in the late 1980s when my parents were still living in that same house, the elms had died from Dutch elm

64

disease. All of their friends had moved away. The large neighborhood shopping center that had seemed so modern and permanent when it was built in the mid-1950s was losing anchor store after anchor store, as it moved from a Gimbels to a Target, to a cavernous empty space with boarded windows. The neighborhood's Jewish anchor had also disappeared. Not long after my parents actually began to attend High Holiday services there, Beth El Ner Tamid, a Conservative congregation and the largest synagogue in the city, which had opened its doors not long before the shopping center, followed its flock to Mequon, a distant, woodsy, up and coming Jewish suburb with large lots, good schools, and streets with exotic names instead of numbers.

Small, nondescript Orthodox *shuls* with their tiny, unimposing entrances and small windows were now the only synagogues left on the West Side. The neighborhood still looked the same. It was still a Chevy and Ford neighborhood. But now many of those Chevys and Fords were owned by black families making their first move out of the inner city and past Twenty-Seventh Street. My old high school, which had only one black student when I attended (at that time the high school less than a mile away from there was almost all black) and had been predominantly white throughout the 1960s, now was majority African American.

On a humid summer night during one of my visits to Milwaukee from Honolulu, my mother and I took a walk through the neighborhood. Fireflies twinkled among the small trees that the city had planted to replace the huge elms. Water from lawn sprinklers danced in the glow of the streetlights. The calls of night birds diving for insects mingled with the quiet voices of people sitting on their front porches drinking beer and lemonade while muted sounds of "The Ten O'Clock News" came through the open windows. Police and fire sirens whooped on the busy street a few blocks away. The walk became a tour, with her as the tour guide to her wayward son from Hawai'i who needed to be brought up to date. As we strolled past the houses, my mother took quick, furtive glances into the windows. She knew the color of every neighbor within a mile of our house.

"This one, they are black. Very nice. Look how nice they keep their lawns."

"That one, whites, look how much crabgrass and dandelions, and look how long the grass is."

"Those blacks across the street, near where Hinterstocker still lives, I don't know. It's July already. Don't you think they could put the snow shovel in the garage where it belongs?"

"Here, this house, he's black, she's white. I think a nice couple but those plastic flamingos. And what's with that pot of dead geraniums?"

"You know," my mother said, "to me it's not whether they are black or white, but do they take care of their place. I don't care what color they are, they can be green with polka dots for all I care, as long as they keep up their homes."

But race mattered more than she admitted. This was not just about lawns and sidewalks. Like it or not, whites moving in said one thing while blacks moving in said something else entirely, something that was not so good and not so promising for old people worrying about crime and thinking of property values when it came time to sell. There were serious struggles over bussing. Crime increased. The neighborhood association fought hard and often successfully in behalf of neighborhood preservation, but it was a constant battle. Now when the *Milwaukee Journal* referred to "The West Side," its readers imagined something different than before. And so did my parents.

Pockets of thriving, prosperous white people with young families were also moving into the neighborhood. My mother would watch them from her living room picture window as they walked past the house. They were Hasids. Since the Twerski *shul* and all the other Orthodox synagogues were still on the West Side, the seriously observant families had to live in our West Side neighborhood so they could walk to *shul* on *Shabbos*, and the number of observant families was growing. Now there were not just a few dressed like Hasids. There were many, including large numbers of young parents who were drawn to Hasidic life as part of the renewal taking place in Jewish communities across the United States. Houses that my parents' friends and neighbors had left years before were filling with bearded young accountants, former *yeshiva bochers* who now sold insurance, and rabbis, all with enormous, young families.

The new Hasidic *reb*, who was one of the old *Reb* Twerski's four sons, bought a house on Fifty-First Boulevard, the fanciest street in the neighborhood. When I was young, the very few Jewish West-Siders who went to prep school all came from that street. But for the Hasids, buying on that street was not snobbishness. It was practicality. They needed big houses for their large families. The new Rabbi Twerski had ten children. Now, since the street had lost its earlier appeal, they could get good space for the dollar. A Jewish day school opened not a quarter of a mile from where the school bus used to pick up those wayward, prep school Jews.

Next door to this day school, the first new kosher butcher shop in Milwaukee in over fifty years opened. No more driving ninety miles to Chicago and coming back with a carload of briskets, ground chuck, and chickens to be stacked in the basement freezer. No more relying on the few stores in Milwaukee that sold Empire

Kosher frozen products. My mother, who had not bought kosher meat for years, began to buy a little ground chuck at this new shop, which was a block from the house. "They are such nasty people," she said about the owners, "but the store is handy, and you can't beat the taste of kosher hamburger meat."

From her living room window, my mother watched those families walking quickly to *shul* to beat the dusk, the father hanging onto his black hat, his unkempt beard blowing in the hard winter wind; the sons in dark gabardine pants, *yarmulkes*, and earmuffs, the beginnings of the boys' side curls clearly showing.

"You know," my mother said to me about these new neighbors, "they are still nuts but at least they are Jewish. It's nice to see little Jewish kids around here again since yours live so far away. And they keep their yards pretty nice, though, to tell you the truth, some of them hire help to do it. But when it snows on *Shabbos*, you better plan on walking on the other side of the street."

More young Jewish families moved in, but old peoples' fears about crime and race were stronger than visions of neighborhood preservation. My parents sold their house and moved to a roomy apartment in Fox Point, an East Side suburb that had always been above my parents' pay grade as long as they had a family to raise.

Next door to them, in a tiny, posh strip mall alongside typically high-end, quasi-hipster suburban businesses — a Japanese restaurant, an independent bookstore, a small dress shop, a coffee house — there was a Hasid storefront *shul*. This was not Those Twerskis. Twerski's synagogue stayed on the West Side, but the Hasid renewal broadened to the suburbs, mainly through the work of the Lubavitchers, the Hasidic sect whose worldwide mission focused on Jewish renewal.

After my father died, my mother moved a couple of miles up the road to Meadowmere, an assisted living facility in Mequon. The Lubavitchers had moved to Mequon too. Their presence had become so strong in Mequon that the Lubavitchers built a community center there, the Peltz Center for Jewish Life. My mother knew nothing about this. She no longer had a neighborhood to worry about. As the Hasidic community became more prominent, she had fallen more deeply into dementia. As my mother stared out of her small apartment window killing time, she saw nothing but a tiny backyard marsh and a few birds in her feeder if she remembered to stock it with seeds, which she rarely did.

The Peltz Center describes its ritual bath as "a tastefully decorated Mikvah. Our Mikvah is flawlessly maintained, fully equipped, and beautifully appointed to make your visit a pleasurable one." More of a suburban spa then a spiritual cleanser. And no polio scare.

Hantzeh's Will

My grandfather Sam Himmelreich summed up his time as a tailor in the Russian Army this way: "The Tsar liked my work so much, that he said, 'Sam, I want you to serve another twenty-five years.' " A nice joke about what would have been a hopeless dilemma: serve the Tsar until Sam was over fifty years old or hide from the Tsar in a place that was more and more risky for Jews. So in about 1900 he, along with all of his seven brothers and sisters, decided to leave Latvia for good.

Most of them chose to come to America, but two of the sisters, Roseh and Hantzeh, decided to go to South Africa instead. South Africa? The rest of the brothers and sisters thought that these two women were crazy. South Africa was the wilderness, the bottom end of the Dark Continent. And what were the chances that all of the brothers and sisters would ever see one another again?

The rest of the Himmelreichs ultimately ended up together in Milwaukee. They became tailors, grocers, and tavern owners. A couple even had some small income properties. Not rich, not poor. But very poor compared to Hantzeh, who became a multimillionaire cattle rancher and salt mine owner.

Hantzeh tried to stay close to her family in Milwaukee. She wrote to them regularly and even invited my mother to come live with her after my mother graduated from high school. Around 1930, more than a quarter century after she had separated from her brothers and sisters, Hantzeh came to that city for a visit. During this safari in reverse, there were some portents that money had already begun to play a role in *Tanteh* Hantzeh's relationship with her poorer brothers and sisters. While at my grandparents' home, Hantzeh asked my mother Celia, who was a young girl at the time, to go buy some nail polish for her. She gave my mother a dollar for the purchase. When my mother returned, Hantzeh asked for the change. My grandmother, who never shirked in her mission to make sure that her relatives knew exactly what she thought of them, said to her rich sister-in-law, "With all the money you have, you are asking Celia to give back the change? What's the matter with you? You should be ashamed of yourself."

No one in the Milwaukee family ever saw Hantzeh in person after her visit. People stayed in touch, but that was all. Hantzeh died in 1961. Her husband had died earlier. After her death, Hantzeh's wealth became a real issue, and not just about change for a dollar. In her will Hantzeh was generous enough to spread some of her wealth among some American relatives. My grandfather and her other brothers and sisters each inherited about $15,000 apiece, a very nice sum at the time; the house he and my parents owned together was not worth much more than that. The anger in the Himmelreich family was not about what *Tanteh* Hantzeh did for her brothers and sisters. It was about what she did for the children of her brothers and sisters, her nieces and nephews who were the Himmelreichs' children: the cousins.

How you treat cousins has been a major marker of proper Jewish family life. "So your daughter Susan is getting married. *Mazel Tov.* Are you inviting the cousins?" There were only two safe answers to this question: (1) yes, all, or (2) no, none. "No, none" means, "It's not possible, we are having a small wedding, only the bride and groom's immediate family." That's okay. Susan's mother and father may be cheap, but at least they are consistently cheap. "We should send a gift anyway. They're entitled."

"Yes" meant every cousin, whether you have not seen them or heard anything about them since your *bris*, whether they are permanent residents of the space station, or whether your feud with their side of the family goes back to an argument over who should go first as the Red Sea parted. Invite. If the cousin does not come, fine. His call, her call, whatever. You are off the hook.

"Be sure to invite your cousin Sheldon."
"He's dead, Ma."
"Better to be safe than sorry."

Hantzeh broke the Cousins Rule. She gave money to two Milwaukee cousins and shut out the rest. The two lucky ones were a brother-in-law and sister-in-law, Marcy and Sol.

"How come Sol and Marcy got when the rest of the cousins didn't?" went the phone conversations. "It's not fair. Okay, maybe Marcy. Her husband, may he rest in peace, died young. Marcy's doing okay what with the apartments she owns. Still, you lose a husband younger than forty to Hodgkin's, you deserve something for your suffering. But Sol? Why Sol? God only knows. He is such a conniver, a *gonif* from the word go."

I can remember no other time when I heard my mother complain about other relatives' money. All kinds of conspiracy theories developed. Sol must have done something to ingratiate himself. Maybe Aunt Ida, who was Hantzeh's sister, Sol's mother, and Marcy's mother-in-law, had a hand in it.

The conflict over Hantzeh's will was in many ways small stuff. It never went public, probably never went outside of the family. No one sued. Ida suffered no repercussions. Marcy ultimately got back in the good graces of the family. Sol, on the other hand, died a *gonif non grata*, but in much of the family's eyes he was already a sleazy outcast before Hantzeh's money became an issue. Sol was Sol. People did not like him before the money. People did not like him after.

Even so, the conflict had a lingering effect. The Hantzeh story became part of Himmelreich lore as an object lesson, part moral and part extremely practical, about what you need to do before you die in order to avoid trouble after you die.

Many years later my widowed mother showed that she had absorbed that lesson. On one of my visits to Milwaukee she took me aside and said sadly, "I made your sister Cheryl executor of my will."

"Fine," I said.

"I just wanted you to know so that you wouldn't be angry," she answered.

"Mom, I live in Honolulu, and Cary [my brother] lives in Toronto. Cheryl lives a mile away from you. She talks to you every day. Of course she should be the executor. What's the problem? She's going to cheat me out of the vast Milner fortune?"

I made fun of what she was trying to do because I was insensitive. I had not absorbed the Hantzeh lesson. My mother made it clearer. "I didn't want you to think I am treating your sister special," she said. Whatever else my mother thought about her death, in her eyes the only way she could ultimately rest in peace was if she died knowing that her will did nothing to upset her children and turn them against one another.

Years before her death my mother-in-law began giving away to her two daughters her silver, dishes, jewelry, and other assorted China cabinet pieces. She said to my wife Joy, "Your sister took some silver platters the last time she was here, so you have to take some Lladró figurines to keep it even. You don't want to take it now? Fine. I'll just put your initial on it with some tape so when the time comes…"

"I don't want to take anything now," Joy answered. "I've got no place to put it. Besides, it makes me nervous talking about this."

"Please. Do it for me. That way, at least I know you and your sister will not fight over it."

There is a good deal of Jewish lore about the spiritual dimensions of death — big picture subjects like reincarnation and the likelihood that your soul will come back to life after the Messiah's return. I never heard anyone in my family talk about those things. Much more practical concerns monopolized their everyday thinking. One was making certain you would have a proper funeral and burial. That was pretty straightforward and easy to take care of in advance.

The second concern was more important and far more complicated than getting a plot, a pine box, and a shroud. Your whole life you work and you work to make sure that your kids get along. They may live far away from each other and not be all that close in the first place, but you keep up the pressure. "When was the last time you talked to your sister?" "Did you remember to send your sister a card?" "You know, you and your sister both, and I really mean both, get more gorgeous as you get older." The real life and death question is: How are you going to keep your money from making things worse between them after you've passed?

The five most reassuring words someone can say about a deceased Jew are not, "May she rest in peace." The most reassuring five words are, "Her kids still get along."

Bridging Troubled Waters

Eddie Fisher got it all wrong. First of all, he jumps the line. No one eats supper at the Forest Trace Retirement Community until three thirty in the afternoon earliest. That's the rule. Before that, you can mill around outside the dining room, schmoozing about today's gossip, current events, or tonight's menu, but you can't go in. Meanwhile it's only three, and Eddie is already eating, courtesy of some toady who thought Fisher deserved special privileges, that he was some big shot just because he recorded "Oh, My Papa" and married all those famous, beautiful *shikses*.

Second, he's doing this in plain view, stuffing himself, *fressing* away like it's going out of style. Even though it's early, there are more people outside the dining room than usual because they have come down to see Fisher in the flesh. And he is late. It's not enough that Eddie is eating in front of everyone as they watch him with lunch counter stool impatience. Worse, Fisher has dilly-dallied so long that he's already cut into his scheduled personal appearance time.

And speaking of appearance, that's another thing Fisher gets wrong here. He's gotten very old looking but still tries to dress like a sharpie, like he's still doing the Copa. He's showing off a two-toned gold and brown sport jacket with matching two-toned tie and shoes. He looks like he's wearing a rug even though he's not.

"What is Fisher, maybe seventy-three, seventy-four?" says a short guy wearing seniors' wraparound shades to protect every millimeter of his eyes from the Florida summer sun. "I'm ninety, and I look better than he does." People laugh in agreement.

And another mistake Eddie makes: When he finally gets down to work, he does not sing a word. In fact he barely talks, and when he does, he mumbles so badly that he is hard to understand even for those few with normal hearing. Guided by the afternoon's hostess, who happened to be the daughter of the famous Jennie Grossinger of Grossinger's Resort in the Catskills, he uses the elegant white piano in the middle of the lounge only to lean on. Eddie says a few words in English, tries out a little Yiddish with a cute grinning style that a sports agent who knows maybe ten Yiddish words would use on his old great-aunt from Lodz. Then Eddie, the poor schmuck, tells an anecdote about Jennie that suggests that at one time he had the hots for her and that maybe they even, you know. This of course embarrasses the daughter, who firmly pulls at Eddie's elbow to get him off stage, which he does after a show biz wink and wave. He does not even remember to say, "You've been a beautiful audience! God bless you!"

No one minds his early exit. The place empties fast. The early bird eaters make their move toward the dining room, which is now serving its salt-free soup, baked tilapia, nova omelets, and non-fat frozen yogurt to everyone, not just to a Mr. Big-Shot-Who-Stuffed-Himself-Early-and-Didn't-Sing-a-Note. The later diners, the ones who dare to eat supper after five o'clock, decide they would rather go upstairs and watch "Three's Company" reruns than hang around this has-been.

This puts a crimp on Eddie's real objective, which was to sell his recently published memoirs. He brought maybe two hundred copies along with him to sign and autograph. Five minutes after he finishes his little talk, the room is deserted with one hundred ninety-seven left unsold.

What was Eddie thinking? Judging from the way he walked and talked, not much, but his real mistake was to take these sophisticated, tough old people for granted. To Fisher, they were simply an "audience" or, more likely, a dim memory of an audience from years gone by. He did not bother to get to know the place. He went out, did hardly any of his shtick, and expected people to fall all over themselves for him. If he had taken five minutes off his unethical dining to get to know these people, he might have connected with them. To him, they were just generic *alteh kakers*, old folks.

But, then, what was Art Garfunkel's problem? After all, he knew Forest Trace. His mother lived there.

The recreation director had hired Art Garfunkel's wife to do a show in the complex's Jennie Grossinger Entertainment Center, Forest Trace's regular concert venue and a larger and more formal room than the one where Eddie appeared. Garfunkel himself decided to do one song, "My Yiddishe Momme," that straight-out, teary tribute to Jewish mothers that Sophie Tucker made famous three-quarters of a century ago.

The audience hated Art's choice. In fairness, a Grossinger Entertainment Center audience is a tough crowd. If they do not like a performer and it's their bedtime, they get up and leave. In fact if they *do* like a performer and it's their bedtime, they get up and leave. But the complaints against Garfunkel were more pointed.

"Why didn't he sing one of his own songs?" my mother-in-law said in her review of his performance. "Every entertainer who comes here sings 'Yiddishe Momme,' " she went on to say with the same disdain she used to describe restaurant food that's too spicy. "Another one, a Broadway singer, was just here. That one started with a nice show tune and then she blended it into 'Yiddishe Momme.' "

To such entertainers, "Yiddishe Momme" may seem to be the generic song for a category called Old Jews, but they have the wrong generation of old Jews. Sophie Tucker made the tune famous in the 1920s. It became the song of the Eastern European immigrants who had come to the US only a few years before. The song reminded them of their own mothers, many of whom were still far away in the Old Country. It was also these immigrants' song because it reflected, at least in their most frustrating parental moments, the way they wanted their smartass modern, first-generation American-born children to think of them — as their *Yiddishe mommes*.

But the people at Forest Trace were not those immigrants. They were the smartass children of those immigrants. The Forest Tracers had been the kids busy becoming modern, first-generation Americans when Sophie recorded the song. They were drinking bootleg whiskey, eating *treif*, learning American slang, and dancing to hot American music, maybe even with a *shikse* if the room was dark enough and they were far enough from home. They were the ones changing their names from Lipshitz to Lipton and from Bornstein to Barnes.

Tucker's song made those young adults uncomfortable because it made their mothers cry like, well, like old Jewish mothers. These children did not always want to be reminded that they had *Yiddishe mommes*. The song made the children feel guilty for not sharing Sophie's sentiments about parents who, to tell the truth, were often a greenhorn pain in the *tuchus*, which often got Americanized to ass. The song made the kids a little edgy. It reminded them just how shaky and vulnerable their new, blended-in status was.

By the time Simon and Garfunkel came along, those children of immigrants were in their fifties, maybe too old to smoke a joint or be a Dead Head, but certainly not too old to know what was what. Their own children bought the Simon and Garfunkel LPs and listened to them at home. The whole family, including the old grandma from the *Yiddishe momme* generation, watched the gawky Jewish boy with the frizzy hair and his cute little Jewish partner with the dark, twinkling eyes sing on the television. And maybe these parents thought that Mrs. Robinson was a slut, a *nafkeh*, for coming on to Dustin Hoffman, but still they saw "The Graduate" or at least knew the song.

Like Fisher, Forest Trace "Yiddishe Momme" singers did not bother to see the difference between old people as flesh and blood and old people as a stereotype. But Garfunkel's reason for choosing that song was different, just the opposite. He chose it because his mother was there. "Yiddishe Momme" was a love song to his mother. It was really a song only for her. In a room full of strangers, Art Garfunkel was a solitary son singing to his mother alone.

Simon and Garfunkel's own songs were as thoughtful as they were beautiful, with elegant metaphors and words that were surprisingly profound for young men, boys really, in their twenties. Even at that age, they sang in "Bridge Over Troubled Water" about the power of being there when someone needs you:

When you're weary
Feeling small
When tears are in your eyes
I will dry them all
I'm on your side
When times get rough
And friends just can't be found
Like a bridge over troubled water
I will lay me down.

Still, this is a song about youth, not about old age and death. The "Silver Girl" who "sails on by" in "The Bridge Over Troubled Water" is not a gray-haired woman whose time has diminished. She is someone whose life lies ahead of her, whose

... time has come to shine
All your dreams are on their way.

And Simon and Garfunkel love songs are about young men's lusty, horny love.

Making love in the afternoon with Cecilia
Up in my bedroom,
I got up to wash my face
When I come back to bed,
Someone's taken my place.

Jubilation,
She loves me again,
I fall on the floor and I'm laughing.

The songwriter and art critic Dave Hickey was only partly right when he said that there are so many love songs because "it's hard to find someone you love, who loves you — but you can begin, at least, by finding someone who loves your love song." It's not just about finding love but keeping it, as the chasms of time and distance get larger. There are so many love songs because the nature of love changes as you go through life. The problem becomes not only finding someone new but holding on to someone old. You may love the same person you always did, but that person's links to your life change dramatically. So you need new love songs.

For Art Garfunkel, "Yiddishe Momme" was a new love song. When he sang at Forest Trace, Garfunkel was a middle-aged man past his prime singing to an old woman who saw him only once in a while on those quick visits to Florida. When a son reaches middle age, both he and his mother realize that they are both in a "hazy shade of winter."

Time,
Time,
Time, see what's become of me
While I looked around for my possibilities.

Former pop star or not, a sixtyish man is a rickety bridge over troubled waters. No bridge, no matter how sturdy, protects a person forever from the roiling, bottomless whirlpools of death.

A middle-aged man looking at his mother puts death in stark relief. When Art Garfunkel sang "Yiddishe Momme" at Forest Trace, he knew that this could be the last time he would ever see his mother. He might not be there when she needed him one last time.

My Yiddishe momme,
I need her more than ever now
My Yiddishe momme
I'd like to kiss her wrinkled brow
I long to hold her hand once more
As in days gone by
And ask her to forgive me
For things I did that made her cry.
Oh, I know that I owe what I am today
To that dear little lady so old and gray.
To that wonderful Yiddishe momme.

Jerry Seinfeld's Florida and My Hawai'i

The stretch of southeastern Florida between North Miami and Boca Raton is crass, noisy, and unattractive. One strip mall follows another. Big Retail is everywhere. Stores shout out their names: Bagelmania, Chair City, and the Great American Smoked Fish Company, which claims to carry "The Biggest Variety of Smoked Fish in the United States of America." Boeing could build its Dreamliner in Sample Road Flea Market's huge, hangar-like building. During Passover the Costco next to that flea market sells paint-can-sized containers of *gefilte* fish.

The weather is unbearably hot in summer, surprisingly cold in winter, and the beaches are only so-so if you can even get access to them at all. Honolulu's beaches and climate beat Florida's hands down. Hawai'i has lush mountains, while South Florida is monotonously flat and non-descript with an overly manicured, artificial greenness. Honolulu feels smaller, older, more exotic. It has far more cachet and far less tumult. Compared to Florida, it costs a fortune to live in Hawai'i, but it is worth the price.

At least through my eyes. I have lived in Honolulu for over forty years, and I formed my impressions of South Florida through the visits to my in-laws who retired to Broward County from Milwaukee in 1967. They first lived in Hollywood, Florida, then just outside of Fort Lauderdale until their deaths almost forty years later.

The Florida that I got to know seemed so Jewish, not contemporary Jewish, but rather parochial Jewish. It reminded me of our family's half-Yiddish arguing and kibitzing sessions at my grandparents' house in Milwaukee in the 1950s. In Florida, shuffleboard games, parking spaces, doctors' offices, restaurants seem to involve discussions with the same cadence, the same volume, all battle cries of everyday life. Even though Jews come from all over the US and Canada to retire there, that corner of Florida felt parochial with a definitely New York Jewish vibe.

There are a few thousand Jews scattered throughout Honolulu but just one temple with a building, along with a Conservative *chavurah* (a communal group that worships without a rabbi) that rents space from the Unitarians. There is also a Chabad outpost that is plucky but miniscule by Lubavitcher standards. There is no Jewish day school, community center, Federation, or Jewish old folks home. No chance of seeing a group of old Jewish guys sitting in a Waikīkī bagel shop kibitzing about their golf game or politics they way they do at Bagelmania because there are now no neighborhood bagel shops in Honolulu. In fact Jews in Honolulu don't gather that way anywhere.

My Florida visits were obligations — part of a considerate son-in-law's tool kit. To pass the time, I became an anthropologist of old Jews. My ethnographic mentors were not Bronislaw Malinowski and Margaret Mead. They were Larry David and Jerry Seinfeld. I was only interested in the funny things that the old people said and did — their shtick. Malinowski never said, "Hey, let me tell you about the Trobrianders' shtick."

My shtick-gathering took place in a square mile area that included parts of Inverness, Tamarac, Sunrise, and Lauderhill. I had regular sites like Bagelmania on University Drive, Flakowitz's Deli, and a nearby strip mall on Forty-Fourth Street where my in-laws regularly shopped. But any place was fair game. The best source of all was Forest Trace, my in-laws' retirement community, which was within the square mile area. Its dining room chats alone could have filled many notebooks.

I used this material in stories, which I told to my friends at parties or to audiences on stage. Like these:

Forest Trace early in the morning. Emergency vehicles, including a fire engine, are in the parking lot as they often are at that time of day when the staff discovers which residents have not woken up. The first responders are there so often that the residents call these emergency vehicles the Forest Trace Taxis. Anyway, an old woman comes out of the main entrance, gets into her Mercedes, and slowly reverses straight back for fifty feet until she broadsides the parked fire engine. She then pulls directly forward until she is back into her parking space, then backs out and does exactly the same thing again.

I got a million of 'em; so let me tell you the one about:

A perfume shop in Shmateh Row (the name alone!), a collection of small discount stores in a run-down strip mall in a desolate, dirt-poor neighborhood in Hollywood. By the way, let me ask you something. What kind of schlemiel would build that thing in that neighborhood? It's like Henny Youngman's brother-in-law opening a tall man's shop in Tokyo. Anyway, an old lady is shpritzing and re-shpritzing a sample bottle of perfume. As the mist spreads throughout the store, she argues with the salesman about whether the discounted perfume is really fresh. "Lady," the salesman finally says, "it's cologne, not fish."

You, the lady over there in the back. Are you okay, sweetie? Good, so would it hurt you to laugh a little? By the way, if those are real, then I'm Francis the Pope. Moving right along:

A former IHOP down the street from Forest Trace and across from a new Chabad synagogue. This diner is now a drab but busy place where you can get two eggs, bagel, and coffee for less than three bucks — egg white omelet fifty cents extra. There are no packets of artificial sweeteners on the tables. The waitresses carry them in their pockets to keep the customers from filling their purses.

Cha ching! I'm on a roll here:

Forty-Fourth Street Shopping Center in Sunrise. After spending close to a half hour in a store that specializes in shoes for the elderly and finding something that seems to be exactly what she wanted, my mother-in-law tells the store owner, who moved his business from New York City because he thought he had found a nice little niche market, that she was not going to take that pair of shoes because they were "too perfect."

Thank you, thank you. You've been a beautiful audience. God bless you and good night.

These stories have legs. They resonate. When people hear them, they knowingly say, "uh huh," as if they understand that this is what South Florida and old Jews are all about. These bits are like the "Seinfeld" Florida episodes, where Jerry visits his parents Helen and Morty at Del Boca Vista.

Tell you the truth, I am tempted to stop right here. Those stories really are funny, and they never fail to work. And who wouldn't want to be like Jerry Seinfeld? So why am I not comfortable just saying that you've been a beautiful audience and exiting stage right? Because there is more to these Florida stories — and less.

These Florida jokes are what we hip, modern insiders tell about those who are no longer on the inside. We are Jerry. They are Morty. We may be just as neurotic as those old people, but in cooler, more nuanced, less trivial ways. A Morty men's group meets at the synagogue on Sunday mornings while a Jerry men's group meets every other Tuesday in a therapist's office or on a long weekend at an elegantly primitive retreat center run by Buddhist monks. We will never sell overcoats for a living like Morty, wear white belts, shout at condo board meetings, or have dinner at four o'clock in the afternoon. Never. Hand to God.

One morning during the summer after my in-laws moved to Forest Trace from their apartment in Hollywood, I was sharing one of the building's elevators with a resident who looked about ninety years old. Because I had just finished a run in the ninety-degree heat, I was shirtless and sweating. When the man stared, I thought he was about to hassle me. Forest Trace was a place that still had a dress code for dinner, after all. Instead, after giving me the once over, he said wistfully, "I used to have a body like yours."

There I was, a man close to sixty with a physique like a vegetarian jogger, whose dating scene had ended without incident in 1965, a person who had managed to walk shirtless on Honolulu beaches for over three decades without anyone, particularly women of any age or eyesight, ever saying anything nice about my body, and now I get this compliment from an osteoporosic old man. But I loved what he said. His words and his look were saying that I was so different from him. I couldn't wait to get back to Hawai'i and tell everybody. I was still a Jerry.

A few years later, after clearing out my father-in-law's apartment, I rode the Forest Trace elevator for the last time. Both in-laws were dead. I no longer had reasons to visit Florida. The source of my material was gone. So was my illusionary defense against growing old.

Those Florida stories were supposed to make me more like Jerry, but in fact their simplicity made me more like Morty. People think that in your sunset years you long for the simple life. That's right in some ways but terribly wrong in others. My main defense against rotting away — the single item in my (I hate the term) bucket list — is this: *Keep life complicated. Continue to embrace complexity. Don't narrow your gaze. Never give up your search for oddity and irony.*

Seeing Florida through the lens of my stories made life too simple for me. It made me an *alteh kaker* observer with rigid tunnel vision. When he was alive, my wife's Uncle Morris would respond to an opposing viewpoint by saying, "don't tell me," as if he already had all the experience and knowledge he was ever going to need. He felt that being old entitled him to his way or the highway. I think he died proud knowing that past the age of fifty-five he never changed his mind about anything important.

That attitude made Uncle Morris old before his time. He was a crotchety pain in the ass.

My preconceptions about Florida made me miss a lot about the other, fuller South Florida. I was not totally clueless. From the same balcony where I saw the old lady hit the fire engine, I regularly saw the many Haitian and Jamaican caregivers arriving at Forest Trace every morning, including the fire engine woman's caregiver who read her the riot act in the parking lot that day. I saw a group of West Indians in white cricket uniforms pass my restaurant table. I ate breakfast down the street from Bagelmania at the Orange Blossom where I had eggs and grits served to me by a waitress who actually had a southern accent. I shopped at a Jewish deli on University Drive that was now owned by a family from India. But Jewish life remained my frame of reference. The Jews were the stars. Everyone else was an extra. In my head, revising the famous "Seinfeld" bit so that Jerry steals a marble rye from a woman in a sari rather than an old Jewish woman would still end up being a story about Jerry Seinfeld. Funny, sure, but that tells you nothing about how the Indian family came to own the deli, which is no doubt a very interesting story and certainly one worth exploring. I could not do standup comedy about this other Florida because I got no material, I tell ya, no material.

Worst of all, I viewed Florida in the same way that I hate about the way so many visitors view Hawai'i. Tourists are full of predispositions about Hawai'i. They know what they want to see before they even arrive and that's what they end up seeing. They follow a lush but narrow path. They eat in Waikīkī and miss the neighborhood restaurants. They go to the North Shore to visit the turtles and surfing beaches but pass right by the vacant pineapple and sugar lands without learning about the significance of those empty spaces and what's beginning to fill them. They are disappointed that Honolulu actually has traffic jams and surprised at how early people here get up and how hard they have to work. They pay to go to commercial luaus but not to see plays about the lives of people who live here. Nothing wrong with this as long as people realize the limits of these experiences. Generally, they don't.

When someone asks me for tips for learning about Hawai'i, the first thing I tell them is, talk less, listen more, and keep your eyes open for those surprising little experiences that pop up. I needed to take my own advice and apply it to Florida. I don't want to turn into an old man riding an elevator who turns to the younger man next to him and says wistfully, "I used to have a nuanced perspective like yours."

Super Bowl *Yahrzeit*

My father's life mirrored the life of the National Football League. Pro football changed as he changed. When my father was growing up in Milwaukee, Curly Lambeau, who coached a team named the Green Bay Packers, which was named after a local meat packing company, took a group of roustabouts and adventurous college boys and built them into one of the early legends of pro football. When Dad was raising children, Packer fans still sat on hard, chipped benches in drafty, rickety stadiums like State Fair Park, a racecar track with high school bleachers. By the time my father retired, there had been more than twenty Super Bowls.

My father did not wear a cheese head or drink coffee out of a helmet-shaped, green and gold Packer mug. But the Packers were woven into the fabric of his life. During his lifetime, he saw all of the Packer greats: Don Hutson, Cecil Isbell, Tony Canadeo, Bart Starr, Brett Favre.

He had a personal tie to another one of these stars, Buckets Goldenberg, a Packer Hall of Famer who along with Sid Luckman was one of the first two Jewish National Football League stars. Buckets played for Green Bay in the '30s and early '40s. He had gone to the same high school as my father and was there at the same time. Goldenberg, an immigrant from Odessa, was a smart, tough ball player who played both running back and guard, offense and defense. Well after Buckets retired, he remained part of my father's ties to the Packers. After his football years, Goldenberg owned and actively managed Pappy's, a very successful restaurant in a Milwaukee suburb located in the heart of the East Side Jewish community. My parents ate there, as did a lot of Packer fans, Jewish or otherwise. Buckets worked the front, so there were always hellos and remembering, and how this guy or that woman was doing. Goldenberg was not a close friend of my father or Dad's brother Eddie, but close enough for a little schmoozing and a quick remembrance. It cemented my father's connection to the team.

My mother was not really a Packer fan. When my dad cheered for the Packers on TV on a Sunday afternoon, she puttered, drank coffee, smoked cigarettes, argued with my grandmother, and maybe made my father a salami sandwich and a cup of coffee. She was proud that Buckets Goldenberg was a star but only in the unanchored way that Jewish immigrants who knew nothing about baseball were proud of Hank Greenberg or the way that Jewish parents, who thought boxing was a brutal, dangerous sport that they would never let their sons do, nevertheless rooted for Slapsie Maxie Rosenbloom and Barney Ross. For my mother it was pride. For my dad it was passion.

When I was younger, I was a Packer fan, too. For a time I even worked for the team, at County Stadium in Milwaukee where Green Bay played a few games each season. I sold hot chocolate to freezing drunks who would pour the steaming, brown liquid onto the cold concrete without drinking it and refill the cups with brandy or peppermint schnapps.

I was in college in Madison during the great Vince Lombardi years. I watched those games on a flickering twelve-inch, black-and-white screen with my roommate, an ex-high school football player who would get so excited before game time that he went around punching people on the shoulder as if both he and his victims were players getting psyched up to take the field. We sang the Packer fight song in front of the TV during every opening kick-off.

After college, as I moved farther and farther away from home, I didn't so much change team loyalties as forget about loyalties completely. I had no favorite team any more. I watched whatever games were on with friends who, like me, now lived far from where they had grown up and learned to be a fan. I experienced the Packers from a long, unemotional distance. Football watching became something clinical, more interesting than inspiring. Living in Honolulu I pretty much got out of the habit entirely. NFL games begin at 7:00 AM Hawai'i Time. There are much better things to do in a perpetually warm and sunny place on a Sunday morning.

My dad died suddenly late in the 1995 NFL season. A few days before his death he had suffered a minor heart attack. He was out of intensive care and was to be sent home in a few days. Instead, the nurses found him lifeless on the floor of his hospital room. When I called my mother to tell her how fast I could get to Milwaukee for the funeral, she was just beginning to try to make sense of the sudden loss of someone she had loved for sixty years. "I can't understand it," she said. "He was doing so well. Just a little earlier in the day he was joking about the Packers."

Almost exactly a year after he died, the Packers won their conference playoff, getting into Super Bowl XXXI, the team's first Super Bowl since Vince Lombardi. "Hey, how about those

Packers!" my mother said to me over the phone on the Sunday this happened.

How about those Packers? I understood what this was about when she then said quietly, "Too bad Dad isn't here to appreciate it."

A week later she said to me, "I think Reggie White is terrific."

"Reggie White?" I said. "What do you know about Reggie White?"

"What do you mean, what do I know about Reggie White? He's my favorite player."

"How can you have a favorite player? In all the years I have known you, you've never paid attention to football."

"You don't know what you are talking about," she said.

So my mother, this eighty-year-old Jewish woman whose sport was mah jong, all of a sudden had a football hero, and he was a six-foot, nine-inch, 325-pound African American male who looked like the person the Milwaukee City Council imagined when they put streetlights in my parents' alley. In fact he looked like the kind of person my parents imagined when they decided to move far away from that neighborhood, new alley lights or not. Plus Reggie was a Pentecostal minister.

My mother was part of a bond that had formed between Reverend Reggie White and Jewish Packer fans well before Super Bowl XXXI. Rabbis seek out complex, important issues with the same enthusiasm as White sought out opposing quarterbacks, so it shouldn't be surprising that Talmudic commentaries have something to say about football. In his lesson on excuses, responsibility, and achievement, the Israeli Talmudic scholar *Rav* Yitzchak Blau, whom no one would accuse of spending time in a Tel Aviv sports bar rooting for the Packers to kick the Bears' asses, offered some powerfully relevant things to say about athletics and theological flexibility. "The athletic team is interested not in acquitting themselves before the heavenly court of sports but rather in winning the game," *Rav* Blau asserts approvingly. "Therefore, they will focus not on justifiable grounds for absolution but how to win games even under the difficult conditions that have presented themselves." Pretty heady language, but all Blau is really saying is what Vince Lombardi had said years before: "Winning isn't everything; it is the only thing."

That kind of thinking was apparent when Wisconsin rabbis were confronted with Reggie White's injury. In 1995, the day before my father's death, White had badly injured his hamstring. White sadly announced that he needed surgery and would miss the rest of the season. But instead, to everyone's amazement, the injury disappeared the next day. Just as you would expect from a Pentecostal, Reverend White said this was a miraculous healing that came about because of his strong faith in God. A Jewish newspaper asked a number of Wisconsin rabbis to comment on this claim.

Now, in the eyes of the rabbis, because he was a born-again Christian, theologically White faced a third down and long. But at the same time he was a star on a team that these same rabbis, not to mention their congregants, cheered for as fiercely as anyone. So the Wisconsin rabbis offered a very measured, Talmudic response to the question about Reggie White's miraculous healing.

Not surprisingly, Green Bay's rabbi, Sidney Vineburg, who could very well be found in a sports bar rooting for the Packers to kick the Bears' asses, gave the most considered answer. Like Rabbi Blau, Rabbi Vineburg cut athletes some slack. Citing an authority that was even higher than God, Vineburg said, "Sources in the

Packers tell me the injury was not as bad as everyone was led to believe." Vineberg did not rule out the possibilities of miraculous healing, but he definitely did not want to get a fifteen-yard penalty for theological interference. Instead he said that there were other explanations for White's healing. Maybe the injury was not so serious, the rabbi said, maybe it had been misdiagnosed. It was not necessarily a miracle. "You want miracles?" Vineburg proclaimed. "If the Packers beat Pittsburgh this week, then we can start talking about miracles." In fact the Packers did beat the Steelers on a dropped Pittsburgh pass in the end zone as the game ended. Do you believe in miracles?

But my mother's bond with White was not really Talmudic. Hers was deeply tragic and personal because Super Bowl XXXI would take place so close to the first anniversary of my father's death. Game day she would be alone with a *Yahrzeit* candle, surrounded by all that excitement and happiness. I thought this would be a very sad time for her.

"How about those Packers!" my mother said happily to me over the phone after the Packers won that Super Bowl. She had watched the whole game at a Super Bowl pizza party given by another widow in her building. My mother cheered the Packers on as she pulled the pork products off her slices.

"You watched, didn't you?" she said to me.

Actually I hadn't. The closer to Super Bowl game day, the more nervous I got. I found myself getting feelings about a team that I had not had for years. I was uncomfortable with this passion. I'd forgotten how to be a fan — or maybe I was just afraid of tapping into those emotions. So I bailed. On Super Bowl Sunday I went to see a film instead, something about ballroom dancing in Japan. It was like being at a League of Women Voters meeting with popcorn.

When my mother asked me if I had watched the game, I suddenly felt disloyal to my dad's memory. If my mother could convince herself that she was a fan now that my father was gone, why didn't I just become a real fan again in Dad's honor and watch the damn game?

I lied to my mother. I told her I had watched. I used ESPN highlights to fake my game analysis with her.

Less than a year later, right before the football season that took the Packers to Super Bowl XXXII, my father's brother Eddie died. Our families were close, more like friends than relatives. For the last ten years of his life Uncle Eddie was in a wheelchair from a stroke that also destroyed his speech and made him weep at unexpected moments. On Saturday afternoons my parents and the rest of the old gang would gather at Eddie and Esther's home to tell the same old stories that they had told for years while Eddie smoked one cigarette after another and cried during the funny parts.

The day the Packers clinched a place in Super Bowl XXXII my mother said to me, "I just finished talking to Aunt Esther." My mother began to cry. Through her tears she said, "We were talking about how much Eddie and your father would have enjoyed this."

Once again, I did not watch the Super Bowl, but my mother did. I lied to her about it just as I had the year before.

To change the subject I asked her, "Did you go to a Super Bowl party this time?"

"No," she answered. "I just sat in the den and watched it alone." Sad words, but surprisingly, she sounded upbeat.

"How come you watched it at all?" I asked.

"Because it's Super Bowl Sunday. What else is there to do? Besides," she said, beginning to laugh, "I may be over eighty, but I still have to be 'with it.'"

Professional Courtesy

The makeshift shelter made it easy to spot my mother-in-law's freshly dug grave. Workers had built a small canopy to protect the few mourners who huddled together in the cold and rain. The rabbi recited the Kaddish and offered shovels to the children and grandchildren so they could begin the final act of covering the casket that had now been lowered into the ground. Milwaukee winter funerals were not new to me. My grandfather had died there on an even colder January day more than thirty years before, and my father had also been buried on a gray, raw December morning like this one. But this time it was different. I was the rabbi. Well, not exactly the rabbi, a rabbi impersonator, an imposter. I lied my way into the job. To understand why, you have to understand corporate America.

I

When my in-laws, Anne and Max Primakow, were growing up in Milwaukee, Jewish funerals were simple there. There were just two Jewish funeral homes, both family-owned, Goodman and Bensman. Both started near one another before the Depression, and each was in the old Jewish neighborhood, within easy mourning distance. There was no problem following the traditional religious law that allows for no more than one day between death and burial because the body lay right there in the neighborhood, and the *Hevra Kaddisha*, the ritual body-washers, were close-by friends or neighbors. Often these rituals were performed when the body was still at home. The deceased's family knew the rabbi, who had probably walked from his house or *shul* to pay his respects and maybe to double-check some eulogy information about a person he already knew pretty well. There was little doubt about who would show up at the funeral, and no doubt at all about who should show up.

The trip to the cemetery took a little while longer because Jewish cemeteries were on the other side of town in gentile neighborhoods where no Jew wanted to live but felt okay with being buried. Still, it was a quick cortege ride, maybe twenty minutes. Returning to their roots for their final resting place was definitely not an option. The old folks may have come from the Old Country and may still have had a lot of greenhorn in them, but, as bewildering as they sometimes found America to be, it was without any question their salvation, their home. So, like my in-laws' parents, they were settled into the ground an easy Sunday drive away. Forever.

But not really forever. The bodies didn't move, but everyone else did. The tightly knit Milwaukee Jewish neighborhood began to spread both east and west. Goodman merged with Bensman to become — and this was even before computer-generated branding — Goodman-Bensman. Not exactly leveraged by junk bonds. Just two guys shouting, "It's a deal! *Mazel Tov!*" Still, these businessmen understood the principles of capital formation and the economies of scale. To get to the heart of the matter, they knew that a monopoly could make more money than an oligopoly.

This new partnership moved out of its two separate quarters and built a plain but dignified new funeral home on Milwaukee's West Side. That's where my in-laws, like the majority of the city's Jews, settled to raise their families. Later Goodman-Bensman added an East Side facility more convenient to the suburban Jews. The partnership flourished, but its job remained the same, burying people who had lived and died in Milwaukee.

But not for long. Milwaukee Jews kept moving, but now to different cities. People no longer were concerned with fleeing from the Cossacks. The children of these immigrants now were concerned with fleeing from the cold. At sixty-two Max gave up practicing medicine and joined this exodus from the tundra. A year after he retired, he and Anne sold their large two-story house on a West Side boulevard and moved to a two-bedroom oceanside apartment in Hollywood, Florida. Just like that. They left Milwaukee forever.

But not really forever. My in-laws, like so many vagabond Jews in Florida, were comfortable living there but not comfortable dying there. For the New York snowbird friends that Max and Anne made in Florida, New York was still the center of the universe and their final home. Florida was a comfortable, low-cost way station to eternity, nothing else. Milwaukee may lack New York City's pizzazz, but for my in-laws the sentimental attachment to Milwaukee was just as strong. They wanted to be buried back there in Spring Hill Cemetery on a small hill alongside my father-in-law's parents.

These modern day funerals are very different. There is no quick hearse ride, no familiar if overbearing rabbi, and no clear list of mourners. The traditional rituals do not lend themselves easily to a two thousand mile trip. To meet this new demand, the funeral industry responded with transportation networks and interstate compacts worthy of UPS and Fed Ex. It was about logistics. After all, from a transport standpoint, moving a body is like moving product and getting the deceased from death to grave requires faster service than even Second Day Air. The need for more complicated arrangements brought heavy hitters into the funeral business. The family-owned funeral homes began to disappear.

It is not easy to "brand" death, but the new industry came up with a term — "northern shipment." South Florida Jewish newspapers like the *Broward County Jewish News* were full of advertisements by funeral home conglomerates offering free Chinese buffet dinners at seminars for elderly Jews who were interested in exploring pre-paid plans for "northern shipment." One took place at Du Barry Chinese, which was close to my in-laws'.

Max bought a plan. But the South Florida siren song "all you can eat!" was not for him. Free lemon chicken or not, he kept his loyalty to his hometown by purchasing a plan from Goodman-Bensman.

At least that is what he thought he was doing. But while he and my mother-in-law were living a full and wonderful life in South Florida, Goodman-Bensman was going through a turmoil that matched a West Texas wildcat oil boom. In 1992 that funeral home became a subsidiary of a company whose name sounds like a NPR corporate sponsor — Loewen Group International. Six years later Loewen sold it to another company, this one with the frighteningly appropriate name Charon, who in Greek mythology was the ferryman of the dead whom the dead person either paid or that poor Greek mortal could not book passage, thus dooming his soul forever. But few mortal souls got aboard the Charon ferry because almost immediately after buying Loewen, Charon flipped it, selling to yet another conglomerate.

So was my father-in-law still doing business with Goodman-Bensman? Yes and no. He was now dealing with, as they say, an entity. While all of this was going on, he got a very reassuring letter from Goodman-Bensman Reincarnated. Every stipulation in his contract would remain valid. But if your bank merges with another bank, is it still the same? Legally, yes, but your own branch might close, or on your monthly statement there may be a new ten-dollar "use of a deposit slip" charge. Still, you use this new bank regularly, so with experience you learn its new quirks firsthand and either accept them or take your money someplace else.

That is definitely not how a person deals with changes in the funeral business. On these matters, the less everyday experience, the better. You don't want to be dropping in regularly on the undertaker to ask, "Hey, what's going down?" As meticulous a planner as Max was, he was still not going to spend time obsessing about an arrangement he considered rock solid. After all, Max purchased the plan so he would not have to think about death any more than an elderly man has to. He paid for silence.

In fact, though, things were anything but financially silent because Goodman-Bensman changed hands again, this time with an ironically nasty twist. A Milwaukee company called Milwaukee Funeral Services (MFS), which for a short time had been Goodman-Bensman's rival, bought the old Goodman-Bensman from the conglomerate. In the 1990s, MFS had been started by a local Jewish entrepreneur who was livid at the price Goodman-Bensman, then already a subsidiary of a large corporation, had charged for his mother-in-law's funeral. So he started his own funeral business right across the street. He advertised cut-rate prices, just as he did with his large, flourishing, inner city clothing store.

But much more was at stake here than the price of Polo knock-offs. He also claimed that Goodman-Bensman violated Jewish rituals by not taking care of the bodies in accordance with the *Hevra Kaddisha*'s body-washing ritual. "They don't have the appropriate refrigeration," he said to a *Milwaukee Journal Sentinel* reporter. "I think they ice the bodies down. That's not the Jewish way. They're not cattle, you know."

Reassuring letter or not, what my father-in-law was unknowingly dealing with was a lot more history, economics, nastiness, and confusion than he had ever anticipated. Had he known, he would have wondered just who in the hell he was doing business with. Knowing Max, if he had any reason to think he should be paying attention, he definitely would have had a Plan B. He never had a chance.

II

My mother-in-law's death came suddenly. One minute my wife Joy was getting ready for work in Honolulu. The next minute she was having a frantic phone conversation with her sister telling Joy that their mother had suffered a stroke and was going to survive for just a few more hours. Only the day before, Joy had had a perfectly normal phone conversation with her mother. Now we quickly needed to answer questions that we had always known would arise but for which we never really prepared. Could Joy make the twelve-hour flight to Florida in time to say good-bye to her mother? Should the grandchildren in Baltimore, New York, and Oregon go to Florida or go directly to Milwaukee for the burial? What should I do?

Max and Anne had made their earlier funeral arrangements with loving but flawed assumptions. When they were in their seventies, it made sense to assume that there were still people living in Milwaukee who would attend their funeral services. But by the time my mother-in-law died twenty years later, Milwaukee was an empty place for them. Almost all their relatives and friends had moved away or died, including the only rabbi they ever had. Anne and Max had lived in Florida for over thirty years. Their friends were now Florida snowbirds like themselves.

At seventy-five, it also had made sense to assume, as both my in-laws had, that either one of them would be at the graveside of the other to say their good-bye. That presence would be the final moment of grace and love together, an indelibly symbolic moment for the one who survived to take back to a now much lonelier life in Florida. Now, at ninety-six with bad knees and a serious heart condition, Max was too frail to make the trip. There had never been plans for a Florida funeral, and Milwaukee was too far away. Max faced the possibility that he would have no chance to say a proper farewell to a woman he had loved for almost three-quarters of a century.

Joy felt a terrible sense of displacement on her flight to Fort Lauderdale. She was a woman in late middle age with adult children of her own, but she felt like a lost child again. One day she is on the phone with her mother and the next... Her father now would be living alone in Florida. What was her role going to be? The burdensome distance between Fort Lauderdale and Honolulu now seemed insurmountable. In the middle of her grieving, she would have to leave her father to travel from Florida to Milwaukee for the funeral, then immediately fly back there to help him. And of course she anguished over her father's problem about the funeral.

Within a few hours of Anne's stroke, with Max too distraught to visit her at the hospital, my brother-in-law and sister-in-law began to put a plan into place. The Baltimore wing of the family, including themselves and their children, would go to Florida. I would fly to Milwaukee to check on the final funeral arrangements there. Our two children would join Joy and me in Milwaukee for the burial. Joy would be the only person in either family to go to both places. Mel, my Baltimore brother-in-law, a nationally known cantor who often presided at funerals, would arrange and conduct a memorial service in Boca Raton. He also became the phone point of contact with Goodman-Bensman.

III

Mel was the crucial link between the new economies of the funeral industry and my rabbinical deceit. Soon after Joy got to Florida, she called me. "Mel's taking care of everything down here. He can't get a straight answer from Goodman-Bensman about whether everything is covered in the prepaid plan, but he thinks they are cheating my father."

"Cheating? How?"

"Mel gets the runaround whenever he asks them about the total cost. They keep saying that they can't tell us yet. It's so hard dealing with them over the phone. He did find out a few things. Mel says that you should officiate the funeral in Milwaukee. He says to tell the Goodman-Bensman people that you are a rabbi. I'll put Mel on the phone."

"Here's the thing," Mel told me. "Max didn't know this when he thought he was all paid up, but Goodman-Bensman adds a four hundred dollars clergy fee unless we furnish the rabbi. So you're going to tell them you're the rabbi."

"You want me to lie about something like that?"

"Sure."

"I don't know. I feel funny about this."

"Come on. It saves four hundred bucks. You know that Anne would have wanted it this way."

I had shopped with my mother-in-law at enough discount places in Shmateh Row and at enough Sample Road flea markets in ninety-degree heat to know that Mel was right on target. Besides, here I was in Honolulu keeping my normal routine, at least for another day, while all of them were struggling so hard in Florida. And my brother-in-law is hinting that I'm chicken. I couldn't say no.

"Okay, I'll do it, but how am I supposed to know what to do?"

"It's easy. When Joy comes to Milwaukee, she'll bring you my book."

Mel's book is small, black, and tattered — probably pre-tattered at the factory to enhance the clerical aura. It is a life stage book — weddings and funerals — similar to ones that clergy of many faiths carry. The book is small because it's bare bones and portable. A rabbi can hold it in one hand while using the other to hold down his *yarmulke* at a garlands, bare-feet, and hand-held-*chuppah* wedding on some gruesomely windy, godforsaken beach. The book has a section for weddings and one for funerals, each clearly marked. Mel marked off the required parts and noted where I had options. In my hands, it would be a "Funerals for Dummies." All I had to do was to remember not to turn to the section marked "Weddings."

At the motel the night before the funeral I studied the book. Mel had marked it as promised. I planned not to press my luck, just simply to stick with the set script. But when I got to one of the options, the Book of Proverbs' "A Woman of Valor," I stopped and read it softly to myself. I wrote "include" lightly in pencil in the margins. Then I practiced reciting the Kaddish over and over. I had said that prayer a thousand times before, but this was different. Words that I usually mumbled through in a crowd became potentially high visibility tongue twisters. Now I would be the enunciator, and others would be the mumblers. Finally I made notes for the eulogy on Residence Inn notepaper with a Residence Inn pen.

The next day, Joy, my children, and I got to the cemetery early to take care of any last minute details. I was hoping there would not be any, but there was sure to be at least one. I parked our rental car next to the funeral director's black sedan a short distance from the gravesite. He and I got out to greet one another in the mist that was beginning to turn to freezing rain. The director expressed his condolences, leaning into our rental Pontiac to make sure Joy could hear him. "Everything is taken care of," he said to her. "Please, you do not have to concern yourselves with any of the arrangements."

Then he said to me, "Who is the rabbi?"

"I am," I said.

He looked directly at me, and I looked back, a stare-down between two *hombres* dressed in black with Boot Hill in the shadows. But no six-guns were drawn. He walked away. He knew. Of course he knew. The brief, hooded expression on his face had told me. But despite my shame about lying to his face in front of God as well as my own grandparents who were buried just a few yards away, I always assumed that I would get away with it, not because he was a yellow-bellied, sap-suckin' coward but because, entity or not, he was a professional. In fact, this man was more than that. He was a *mensch*, a real *mensch*. He was not about to haggle over credentials at a time like this.

The four of us silently walked the few muddy yards and joined the others who were already seated under the canopy. I sat Joy down in front, squeezed her hand, glanced at my children flanking her, and went up to the small podium to begin. I looked out at the small number of mourners — two of Anne's cousins who still remained in the city, some of our old West Side friends, and my aunt with her eighty-seven-year-old boyfriend. I took a breath and reminded myself to go slowly.

So it was then that this shepherd first called out to his flock.

And his flock responded:

"Louder!"

What an amateur I was. Any real rabbi would know that the first rule of worship when old people are in the audience is, "Thou shalt raise thine voice to the heavens!"

When it was time for my eulogy, I looked down at my notes then pushed them aside. It was just too cold to keep people any longer.

I carefully recited the Kaddish, stumbling once, and then sprinkled a packet of Israeli soil into the lowered casket. My family, followed by the others, shoveled dirt into the grave. We stayed there for a moment, Joy longer than the others.

As we said our good-byes to the mourners, my aunt hugged me and said, "You did good, but don't give up your day job." I went over to thank the funeral director, but I did not linger. He acted like he did not expect me to.

A few hours later the four of us scattered again. As the sun came up at O'Hare, Joy and I hugged good-bye.

She called me from Florida the next day. "Is everything finally taken care of with Goodman-Bensman?" I asked.

"Not yet. There are two additional charges. One is a hundred-fifty dollar charge for a 'seasonal digging fee.' "

"Seasonal digging fee?"

"It's an extra charge for grave digging because the ground was frozen."

I pictured my brother-in-law ordering me to put on a hard hat, grab a pickaxe, and further honor Anne's memory. "Hey, buddy, cold enough for ya? Local Seven sent me down here to dig the Primakow grave. You know, I could really use a cup of fresh coffee, and are those doughnuts?"

"And there's this one other charge," Joy said.

"For what this time?"

"Three hundred dollars because my mother was not a member of B'nai B'rith. My father can't remember if she was a member or not, and we can't find any proof. I've been looking through her old magazines. Lots of *Hadassahs* but no *B'nai B'riths*."

"She wasn't a member of NASCAR either. Are they going to charge your father for that, too? Doesn't this sound screwy to you? Why would they penalize someone for not being a member, instead of giving a deduction for being a member when a person buys the plan?"

"I don't know. Mel says to let it go. We're all too exhausted to find out."

Walmart Greeter: A Step Up for the Successful Professional

When highly paid professionals like many of my friends talk about retiring, they often say, "Maybe I'll become a Walmart greeter." They do this with an ironic smirk and a chuckle as if it's the last thing they want to do. They are wrong. It should be the first thing because Walmart will be the best job they ever had. Here are four reasons why.

1. You only have to be nice to your customers for five seconds tops.

To be ethical and to make money, professionals like doctors, lawyers, and financial analysts have to do complicated things with their clients, things that take a long time. Think of this PowerPoint bullet that could be a part of any professional training:

> Professionals *must* foster *ongoing relationships* with clients
> or patients, working hand in hand with the client to *develop
> long-term horizons and objectives* that must be *systematically
> monitored and managed.*

In other words, you have to spend huge amounts of time with rude, stupid, and venal people who you can't kick out of your office because (a) they pay your mortgage and, much worse, (b) your actual job is to take the time to rid these people of the same things that make you crazy when you have to deal with them.

All your professional life instead of telling a client to buzz off, you have had to *mutually problem-solve, listen with empathy,* and *get to yes.* You have been doing this over and over again day in and day out every freaking day of your professional life. And the last few years this has been getting worse, right? You've been accumulating wisdom doing your highly skilled job for close to forty years — nuanced knowledge, informed intuition, know-how, the culmination of your life's work — and some schmuck of a client tells you that he has a much better idea. You are tired of hearing some passive aggressive idiot's theories about why his wife hates him, or how a 188/120 blood pressure is okay because his great granddad on his mom's side lived to ninety-five, or how her Jack Russell can choose annuities by wagging his tail. How many times did you want to say, "Hey, dickhead. Fuck off and die." How many times did you actually say it? Enough with the stifling already. Liberate yourself at Walmart. How long does it take to say, "Diapers? Aisle 6." End of story. You've done your job, you're off the hook. Cha ching. Next.

2. And yet those five seconds include just enough intimacy.

Intimacy: Professionally you want it, you need it, but it can get you into deep doo-doo. Getting close to your clients or patients is key to your job, but it's also a minefield. How much? How far? How close? What if? If some morning before work you are waiting in the Starbucks line and one of your colleagues turns to you and says, "I hear that Chuck has been intimate with a couple of his clients," what would that suggest to you? Exactly. I used to be a college professor. If someone had ever caught me hugging a student, *mucho mucho pronto* I'd find myself in the gender equity officer's suite doing two hundred one-armed, punitive pushups while she signed me up for three consecutive, mandatory all-day Saturday workshops. And that's the best-case scenario.

Still, what about the closeness you feel to your clients? What if they badly need support or a shoulder to cry on? What if some of them are also your friends? What if it's your secretary's birthday, but she has only worked in the office for a week? What if, what if. You've spent your entire career warily weaving through this treacherous sexual harassment thicket. So now's the time to liberate yourself. A Walmart greeter is supposed to hug! The Walmart hug is short enough to avoid trouble but just long enough to satisfy your need for acceptance and contact.

And you get to wear a smock, which, let's face it, is no less stylish than those monotonously muted aloha shirts or the blue button-down Oxford cloth dress shirt with the rolled-up sleeves and the too-tight-in-the-waist-and-thigh relaxed-fit Perma-pressed Dockers that you wear each Casual Friday. With Top-Siders? Really? In 2013? And physicians, you are simply replacing a white smock with one that is livelier, roomier, and better for hiding dirt. Face it, men. You've become too old, too bald, and too fat to be hip, so embrace the smock.

3. You can drive, you can park.

Over the years, way too much of your hard-earned money has gone to pay monthly parking fees large enough to float the Greek debt. Or maybe instead you van-pool, spending two hours each day imprisoned in a Toyota mini-van with a guy's secret smoker breath, a woman obsessing over getting her daughter whose SAT score is lower than her body temperature into Stanford, and a driver who wouldn't take an alternate route if he were on a collision course with a tsunami. Working at Walmart, you can drive to the job. By yourself. And park. For free. Space? A Walmart lot can hold the entire 101st Airborne with room to spare for a battalion of partially trained Afghan soldiers. And accommodating? Walmart lets RV owners park for free overnight. RV owners!

4. Best of all, you free yourself from yourself.

Why put being a Walmart greeter on your bucket list if the pay is so bad? Well, it's not about the money. It's about aspirations. There aren't any. Face it, the last few years as you approached retirement, you've been obsessing over this: "I should have (fill in the blank with your own particular source of insecurity), but now it's too late." That's right, it is too late. So let it go. You've done well. Or good enough. Or at least better than your law school classmate who's the repo specialist. Go to the light. Move on to Walmart where doing a good day's honest, straightforward work is all the accomplishment you need.

Wait a minute. That sounds like your father's old job, the one that got you through college.

Planning for the Past

The old-timer immigrants in the Himmelreich family didn't retire. They quit work. Quitting work is straightforward and simple: Q. "Hey, Uncle Itzeh, when are you finally gonna quit work?" A. "End of July." End of story.

Retirement, on the other hand, is complex and uncertain: Q. "Hey, when are you finally going to retire?" A. "Oh my God, I don't know. It depends on so many, many, you know, variables. On the one hand, there's the possibility that…" Retirement is not the end of the story. It is just the beginning.

Quitting work is old-fashioned, blunt, and has a take-this-job-and-shove-it vibe. Retiring is modern, nuanced, and oh so existential. Because I used to be a college professor, nuance and existential are key parts of my tool kit. I never leave home without them. Around the time that I first began to think about retiring, I was at a Starbucks leafing through a copy of a new book by a colleague of mine. I was not surprised that he sent me a complimentary copy because I had commented on an earlier draft, but I was caught off guard by what he had written in the inside cover: "You are such an important figure in my world, not just for the insights and acumen, but for the life fully lived and enjoyed."

Normally I would have seen this simply as a nice compliment, the same way I thought about a student telling me that I was a good teacher. You take the compliment at face value — why not? — then move on. My reaction this time was totally different. Face value, are you kidding me? I found myself converting my colleague's compliment into an exam question about my life and worth. Had I really lived — was I living — a life fully lived and enjoyed? Was I authentic? I teared up. Thinking about retirement had raised the ante.

The hardest thing about retiring is not the money. It's the deep, deep questions I am supposed to answer. What kind of person am I? What kind of person do I want to be? How close do I want to live to my children? How close do they want to live to me? Is retirement a time to slow down, withdraw, and reflect? Is it a time for more adventure? On my eightieth birthday should I sleep late or sky dive? Is it now time to give back to others? To take more from others?

Plus Alzheimer's, Alzheimer's, Alzheimer's, Alzheimer's and the things I should do to stave it off — Sudoko, chair exercises, taking on intellectually challenging projects like, say, writing a self-absorbed essay about retirement.

Those questions are a burden, a millstone. They are impossible to answer. Thinking about them wastes time, fosters fear, and uncovers concerns about my self-worth that had been nicely suppressed for a long time. So why put yourself through this torture? Because nowadays everyone who's thinking about retiring is supposed to consider these questions. You are an improperly aging person if you don't. If you don't take these questions on, at best you are irresponsible or in denial, and at worst, well, God only knows. The morality of aging: aspire and plan, aspire and plan. Do not dawdle. Never sit still.

Retirement planning has become an industry that's geared to force an old person to produce a road map of the rest of her life. Financial planners now call themselves retirement coaches. Exactly. It's like Congress passed a No Geezers Left Behind law, and we old folks need to take the test. That's why a bucket list is the Boy Scout handbook of aspiring seniors — a merit badge in educational cruises, another in trekking in Nepal, another in social network expansion. And there is so much study material: TV ads, DVDs, Sunday supplement magazines, workshops, personal goals, personal trainers, probability graphs, NPR — experts teaching us how to grow old. People who haven't prayed since their mom made them say grace at grandma and grandpa's house fifty Thanksgivings ago decide to get involved with some religion — any religion — because research says that it will make you live longer. "Wicca, what's their life expectancy?" Old-time religion was about preparing to meet your maker. Retirement-planning religion is about staving your maker off.

This barrage of information is supposed to make me feel secure. In fact it makes me feel vulnerable. Getting old properly is a full time job, and I am afraid that I am not putting in the work.

For those Himmelreich old-timers, those big questions would have been more than a waste of time. They would have been inconceivable. The old-timers did not think about how close they should live to their kids because for years before they quit working, they were already living with them — close families, one bathroom. They owned these homes with their children, so after retirement the old folks were not going anywhere. For that generation moving to Florida was as likely as colonizing Mars.

Financial planners? Why would they need one? The old-timers had nothing to invest. They bought Israel Bonds and US Savings

Bonds, but that was about attachment, not investment. Besides, the Depression had taught these immigrants all that they needed to know about financial planning: *When it comes to money, save what you can and always be looking over your shoulder.*

Challenge? Adventure? Those folks had run away from pogroms, deserted the Tsar's army, struggled to learn the customs and language of a totally strange place, busted their chops hanging on to their homes during the Depression, watched with powerful but mixed emotions as their children became American and their grandchildren became even more American, and witnessed the destruction of six million Jews, including some of their relatives. They did all this while working in their taverns, groceries, and tailor shops six days a week year in and year out and without paid vacations. What they wanted after they quit work was their own personal Elder Hostel tour: to sit in the back yard in their short sleeve shirts, suit pants, and fedoras, kibitzing and drinking Minute Maid Frozen Lemonade if the Frigidaire was working well enough to make ice.

My father Dave was different from these old-timers in some very obvious ways. He was born in America and had a couple of years of college. He looked like Gregory Peck. The Himmelreichs looked like the cast of "Fiddler on the Roof." But like the old-timers my father learned his economics from the Depression. When it came to work, his life was remarkably like theirs. So was his retirement.

Beginning in the late 1930s, Dave drove a laundry truck six days a week for close to fifty years. Well into his seventies he was still delivering large bundles of laundry on below zero days in bad neighborhoods. Technically he was a small business owner, but the business was as small as it could possibly get. He had no employees. He had no building. He had one truck, which doubled as our family car.

He saved money Depression-style. Every night he would put that day's receipts into envelopes categorized by things he needed to save for — "truck"; "insurance." There was no envelope marked "discretionary income."

My dad did have two retirement coaches during his lifetime, but not the official kind. One was his shifty brother-in-law Hy. Every so often over the years, Hy tried to unload one of his taverns on my father. "Take it, Dave!" Hy would say. "*Boychik*, get yourself out of that *farkuckteh* truck once and for all."

At the time, Milwaukee was full of neighborhood mom and pop taverns. Parents took their children to these places. The kids drank orange soda while the parents drank beer and brandy. They all shared the pretzels, hardboiled eggs, and pickled pigs feet. That was definitely not Hy's business model. His bars were dark, seedy caves. Ripped stuffing stuck out of his bar stools. Tough, coarse guys went there to drink when they wanted to escape from mom and pop and spend some time with a girl named Sugar.

My father never seriously considered these offers. He was not about to take a risky new job when he already had a steady job. Like the old folks, he also had learned another lesson from the Depression: *Don't give up a steady job for a new job because…* *you just never know.*

Soon after my father finally quit the laundry business, he took a job selling hats and gloves at Donges Gloves, an old, established family business still holding its own in a shabby neighborhood near downtown Milwaukee. Working in a haberdashery was definitely not part of my dad's bucket list. Donges was not part of any road map or adventure. Dave did not sell Kangols to

African American hipsters as a way of giving back to the minority community. He went back to work because he needed the money but also because working was so much a part of him. Working steady steadied him.

At that time my dad could not legally work at all because he was collecting full Social Security benefits. He was right at home at Donges because the entire sales staff was old and cheating. The owner of the store, Jerry Kahn, was even older than his staff of retirees. As a manager of employees, Kahn was an eighty-something Jewish Mister Dithers.

Kahn himself turned out to be my dad's other retirement coach. When my father was over eighty and still putting in time at Donges, he had a stroke. It did no permanent damage but kept him out of work for a few months while he went through rehab. When my father was ready to return, he called Kahn and asked for his job back.

"No way," Jerry said. "You're not coming back unless you get yourself a hearing aid."

My father had been hard of hearing for years. He paid no attention to anyone — doctors, wife, children — who tried to convince him that he had a hearing problem that was isolating him from conversation. Deep down we all worried that this isolation was the first step toward Alzheimer's.

For my father a hearing aid was too visible a sign of growing old, and that made him feel very vulnerable. So he blamed the problem on earwax.

Kahn's threat about the hearing aid humiliated my father. He refused to talk about the phone call even with my mother. But a short time after the call, Dad went out, bought himself a hearing aid, and went back to work. He died a few months after that.

I heard about a retired college professor who became so insecure about his worth that he polled all of his former grad students, asking them what they thought of him. Imagine my grandfather Sam calling any of his old customers to ask if the alterations held up on the bar mitzvah pants he had shortened in 1951:

On the scale one through five, what is your opinion of the following: "Sam, you made the pants too long."

Or my father surveying his customers:

In 1969 you had an interaction with Milner's Home Laundry regarding dry cleaning spots on your son's only pair of good pants that he planned to wear at his cousin's bar mitzvah the next day. I'd like to ask you some brief questions about that interaction. This call may be monitored.

In a way, though, my father and I are the same because old age made both of us feel so vulnerable. But our vulnerability was propelled by different questions. His was "How do I keep doing what I was doing?" Caution. Mine is "Where do I go from here?" Options.

I live in a bubble of privilege. My father did not. Yet he lived the last part of his life pretty close to his expectations. His was a bubble of consistency. Nowadays there may no longer be a protective bubble at all. Today people who had assumed that down the road their retirement would be as good or better than their parents' fear that they may not have even as much as those old immigrants did. I'm talking about my children's generation here.

Talk about your tears.

Made in the USA
Charleston, SC
04 October 2013